Fabulous Bags
to Stitch & Make

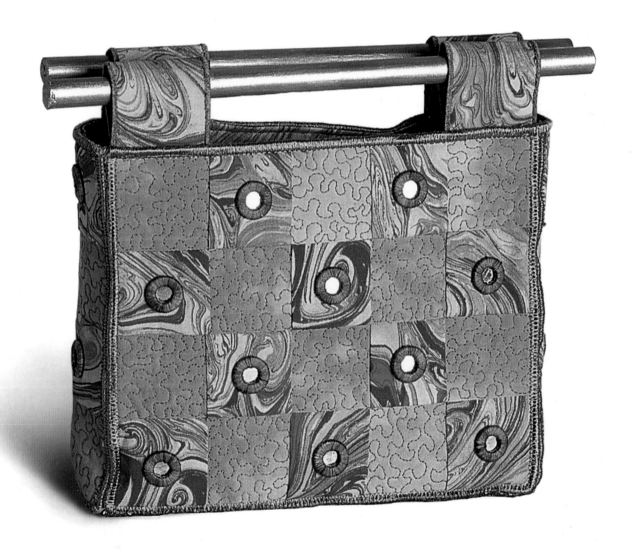

First published in Great Britain 2009

Search Press Limited
Wellwood, North Farm Road,
Tunbridge Wells, Kent TN2 3DR

Based on the following books published by
Search Press:
Handmade Embroidered Bags by Jenny Rolfe, 2005
Handmade Embroidered Purses Using Free Machine
Embroidery by Jenny Rolfe, 2007

Reprinted 2010

Text copyright © Jenny Rolfe 2009

Photographs by Charlotte de la Bédoyère,
Search Press Studios, and by
Roddy Paine Photographic Studios
Photographs and design copyright
© Search Press Ltd 2009

ISBN 978 1 84448 393 8

Suppliers
If you have difficulty in obtaining any of the
materials and equipment mentioned in this book,
then please visit the Search Press website: www.
searchpress.com

Publisher's note
All the step-by-step photographs in this book
feature the author, Jenny Rolfe, demonstrating
the making of embroidered bags and purses.
No models have been used.

For Barry, my husband and best friend.

Acknowledgements

*I would like thank The Bramble Patch and Arterial of
Cosby for supplying a lot of the fabrics, threads and
beads used in this book. Thanks also to Oliver Twists
for decorative threads and craftynotions.com for
bondable fibres and threads among other things.*

*I would also like to thank European Quilting Supplies
Ltd of Leicester, who supply YLI threads to shops
throughout the UK, for supplying them to me as well!*

*For helping to proofread my projects, thanks to my
friends, Claire Higgott and Carole Wood.*

*Special thanks to my daughter Tiffany for her
encouragement and support and to my son, Ashley,
for helping me to understand my computer.*

*Finally thanks to everyone at Search Press,
particularly Roz Dace and also Sophie and Juan
for making it all come together, and Roddy for the
wonderful photography.*

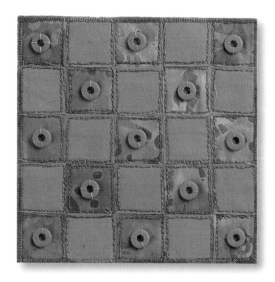

Fabulous Bags
to Stitch & Make

Jenny Rolfe

SEARCH PRESS

Contents

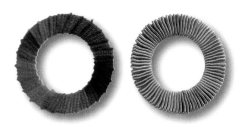

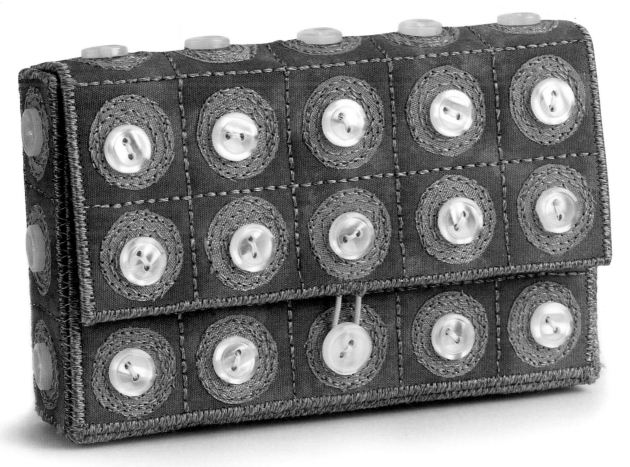

Introduction

I have in the past predominantly been a quilter and as such the idea of sitting in front of the fire in the winter, snuggling under a quilt whilst hand stitching it is an appealing one. However, when I had more quilts than beds to put them on, I decided to down-size and started making smaller hangings which increasingly incorporated my second love: embroidery. Then I only had so many walls to hang them on, so I had to down-size further!

As bags have been a passion of mine for many years, it seemed a good idea to make my own: you can never have too many bags! I could never find quite what I wanted in the shops. I do find, however, that I still have to go shopping on a regular basis: I tell my husband this is 'research'. Although these days it is easier to find embroidered bags, there is nothing quite like making your own, as you can put your own unique stamp on them. The bags in this book are all made using free machine embroidery, but do not worry if you have not done this before. I will take you through the basics and show you examples of different stitches and you can let your imagination do the rest.

It is a misconception that you have to have a top of the range sewing machine for free machine embroidery. As long as you can lower the feed dogs or cover them with a plate, you can free machine, however old your sewing machine. It does, of course, take practice, but then so do most things in life. I still sit in front of the fire on a cold winter's night, but now I am adding beads and hand embroidery to my machine-embroidered pieces. Go through your stash of fabrics and bits and pieces that you have bought at shows, taken home and then realised you had no idea what to do with: they can be incorporated in your bag designs. The important thing is to enjoy making the bags. I hope you will be inspired by this book and will enjoy making your own unique bags and purses.

Materials
Fabric

A lot of the fabrics used to make these bags and purses can be found at your local quilt or haberdashery shop, such as cottons and silks. You may have to go further afield for different textured fabrics such as metallic organza, chiffon, velvet and netting, although they are becoming more and more available. Half the fun is searching through your stash of bits and pieces that you have bought at quilt and embroidery shows.

A selection of different fabrics.

Threads

Machine quilting threads There are many on the market – I like to use the variegated ones. They are usually made from cotton.

Machine embroidery threads Many of these are made from rayon and give a lovely sheen to your surface. They come in many colours.

Metallic threads These are very useful and add texture to your sewing. If you sew quite densely, they catch the light wonderfully.

Invisible thread This is very useful and comes in light and dark. Even threads that are too thick to be used on the top of your sewing machine may be used on the bobbin, and you then sew on the reverse of your fabric, using an invisible thread on the top.

Hand embroidery threads These can be used to enhance your surfaces by couching down, French knots etc. They can also be used to make tassels and covered cords. Crochet threads, perlé, fine ribbons, cords and cotton à broder will all come in handy.

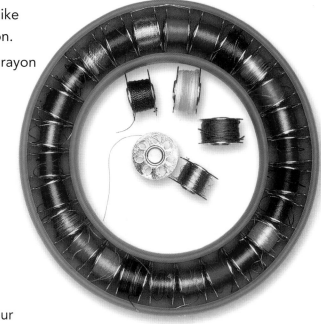

Threads of various types and colours.

Sewing machine

A basic sewing machine is all you need – as long as you can either lower the feed dogs or cover the plate, you are ready to go. Keep your machine clean and oiled (if appropriate) at all times – it is amazing how quickly the bobbin area gets clogged up. For the purposes of this book a darning (or open embroidery foot) is essential for free machining. An appliqué foot, which is open at the front so you can see what you are sewing, is not essential but really useful.

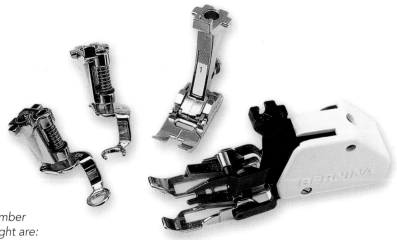

Your machine will come with a number of feet. Shown here from left to right are: a basic darning foot for free machining; a similar foot with an open front for free machining; a basic foot for straight stitching and a walking foot which helps to feed the fabric through evenly, making difficult fabrics much easier to sew.

Basic sewing equipment

Scissors You will need a small, sharp, pointed pair for cutting threads and a larger pair for cutting fabrics. Curved scissors are useful but not essential and are used for snipping threads in awkward places. Most importantly keep a pair just for cutting paper and don't let anyone else use your best scissors!

Pins I like to use the flower-headed variety – they are very long and sharp and if I drop any on the floor I can find them easily (very useful when you have animals or small children in the house).

Machine needles I keep a selection of needles – I tend to buy them when I see them in the same way that I buy threads. There are so many needles that you can buy for specific purposes i.e. 'quilting needles', 'metallic needles' and 'denim needles', but I find that top stitch needles are good for most machining purposes including free machining, as they have long eyes and threads don't break as easily. A selection of sizes 80–100 is probably all you will need to start with and as with threads, you can add to them when you see them. The most important thing to remember is that needles can blunt very quickly and need to be replaced frequently – don't wait until they snag your fabric.

Crewel needles For hand stitching, a packet of crewel needles in various sizes should start you off and you can add to these when you need to use very fine or very thick threads.

Curved needles These are useful for sewing rigid edges.

Other useful items include a **seam ripper** for undoing any sewing, a tape measure and thimbles.

Pins; dressmaking, paper and embroidery scissors; seam ripper; tape measure; crewel needles; thimbles; machine needles; sharps and curved needles.

Embellishments

Beads and sequins in all shapes and sizes can be used to embellish your bags and purses. Shisha glass adds a bit of shine and you can make your own by covering washers in threads to match your bag. Hardware shops are interesting places to search around for some of these items and you could also look there for wire in different sizes. Wire can be made into wired covered cords which can then be couched down on to fabric. It can also be threaded with beads and sewn on to a background. Hollow plastic tubing bought from medical suppliers and filled with beads can be used for bag handles, as can plastic bangles or pieces of dowelling. Ribbons can be couched down as a background and come in a variety of colours, patterns and widths. Buckles can be sewn on to the purses and brooches can be pinned on with safety pins. Even zips do not have to be boring: you can make them a feature and then look around for charms which can be attached to the ends using split rings. Magnetic clasps can be added for extra security. I love buttons and you can add them to any of the purses or even completely cover a purse with them. Bondable fibres are fibres that bond together when heated to make a shiny fabric. You can create some wonderful effects with these fibres, as shown on pages 32–33.

Beads, sequins, shisha mirrors, wire in various colours, washers and covered washers, all used for embellishing bags.

Right, clockwise from top right: bondable fibres, charms, buckles, magnetic clasps, buttons, zips and ribbons.

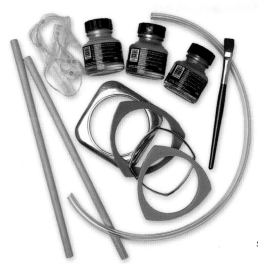

Left: hollow plastic tubing, dowelling and bangles for making handles, acrylic paints and a paint brush for painting wooden handles and sequinned ribbon to trim embroidered bags.

Other items

Fusible webbing This is used to bond two fabrics together. It has a non-stick paper backing which can be used for tracing patterns and is ideal for appliqué. Fix using an **iron**.

Baking parchment (Not greaseproof paper.) This is used to protect your iron.

Fabric glue sticks, fabric adhesive spray, PVA glue and a spatula All useful to keep your pieces of fabric where you want them to be.

Pegs and weights Used to hold parts of bags together while glue dries.

Water soluble film Used on an embroidery frame to create lacy patterns that interlock. When you have finished sewing, you dissolve the film using hot or cold water, and the stitching, once dry, can be sewn on to a background.

Mount board This is very thick card. It can be used as a base for more structured bags and can also be used for winding thread on to make tassels. Always cut it with a craft knife on a cutting mat.

Pencil, eraser and double-sided tape For making templates and designing.

Wire cutters Used to cut wire for embellishing bags.

Ruler This is essential. I like the ones used in conjunction with rotary cutters as they come in a variety of lengths and widths, have grid marks printed on them and are see-through. However, any ruler will do.

Heavyweight interfacing This is used to give shape to structured bags.

Quilting gloves These are thin gloves that have rubber tips to keep your fabric taut when you are free machine sewing.

Felt This is used as the inside layer of the bags.

String Used for making covered cords (see pages 36–37).

Wadding/batting Natural cotton wadding works well and is nice and flat.

Freezer paper This is a waxy paper that can be cut into shapes, ironed on to fabric as a template and then sewn round.

Round-nosed pliers For fitting magnetic clasps.

Shirring elastic This is used to make fastenings.

Clockwise from top left: heavyweight interfacing, fusible webbing, baking parchment, iron, spray adhesive, PVA glue, fabric glue stick, spatula, pencil sharpener, eraser, wire cutters, cutting mat, mount board, rotary cutter's ruler, craft knife, water soluble film on an embroidery frame, pens for marking fabric, pencil, pegs, weights, quilting gloves, double-sided tape, felt, string and thin water soluble film.

Design

Three elements are particularly important when you are designing quilted fabric projects like embroidered bags and purses: colour, shape and texture.

For colour, I find that nature is a particularly good source of inspiration: think of spring flowers, summer skies, green fields and leaves as they turn in the autumn.

I like to work with basic shapes such as squares and circles. These are wonderful when repeated or distorted: think of a piece of wire mesh and how you can bend and change it.

Buy a small notebook and every time you see an image that captures your imagination in a magazine or elsewhere, stick it in your notebook. You will soon see a pattern emerging and realize that you are drawn by certain colours and shapes.

Texture is important when it comes to translating your sketches into stitches. This is why I like to work with basic shapes: their simplicity leaves me free to go over the top with texture when stitching and sewing.

When you are out walking, keep an eye out for fallen leaves. They don't need to be perfect – in fact they are more interesting when they have a few holes.

I am particularly interested in seed heads – cowslip, hogweed or poppy – and I like to interpret them in machine embroidery. I go out for walks in the country and come back with all sorts of seed heads which I dry and then put them in my sketchbook for future reference. You can see how this led to the free machined design on the Clutch Purse shown on pages 110–115.

Poppy seed heads are a wonderful shape and texture. I sketched these in pencil and then added a wash with water soluble pencils. Finally I hand stitched a small sample on fabric.

I like to keep samples of old, unusual and foreign textiles for reference. I make notes in my sketchbook to remind me of where they came from.

In the scrapbook shown below, the fabrics on the left and at the bottom right are from India and the one on the top right is silk Kente cloth from Ghana.

For one of the projects in this book, I decided to make an Indian purse (see pages 92–99). The design was partly inspired by Indian bags and fabrics I found in local shops. Prompted by these and other influences, I set to work creating my own Indian designs in my scrapbook.

Indian bags that helped to inspire one of my purses.

16

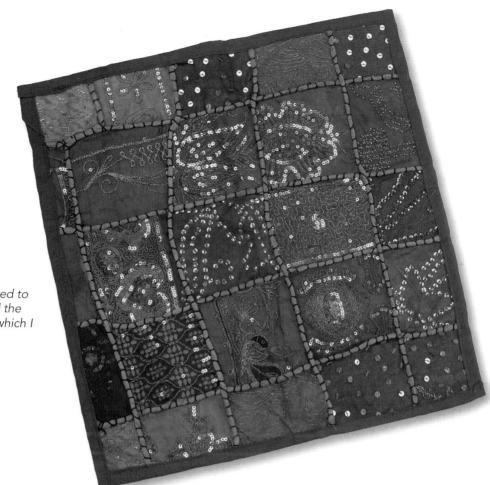

Some of the fabric that helped to inspire my Indian Purse, and the pages of my scrapbook on which I worked on the design.

How to start

I love nothing more than getting all my fabrics and threads out at the start of a project. I keep special threads such as machine quilting threads, machine embroidery threads, metallics and rayons in large baskets. I divide them into warm colours: reds, oranges, yellows; neutral colours such as creams, browns, gold, bronze and copper and cool colours like blues, purples and greens. I have other baskets devoted to thicker threads, cords and braids and ribbons in a variety of colours and also beads and sequins and wires.

I keep my cotton fabrics divided into colours and keep special fabrics such as organza, chiffon, velvet, netting and silk together in all different colours.

When I have decided what colour palette I want to use for the new project, I pull out fabrics, threads and beads from every basket and set them out in front of me. This in itself is very inspirational.

These are typical selections from my fabrics and threads, which I have divided into warm, neutral and cool colours.

Here, inspired by the page from my sketchbook shown below, I have chosen threads and fabrics from the 'cool' themed basket, and decorative threads and ribbons to complement them.

I use pencils and water soluble crayons in my sketches to work on the shapes and colour schemes that inspire me.

I then like to make up free machined fabrics in similar colour ways, for instance, all green to all blue, for use in my projects.

I choose threads, beads and embellishments to complete the look.

Techniques
Free machining

This technique might seem complicated at first but once mastered, opens up infinite possibilities. You are in control of the stitching – you can go in any direction, not just forwards. With most machines you need to lower your feed dogs and replace your standard foot with a darning foot. You will need to refer to your sewing machine manual if you need to cover the feed dogs with a plate.

Turn the stitch length and width to 0.

Before embarking on any project you should make sure that your tension is correct. You might need to lower the top tension; do this a little at a time.

Remember that if the bobbin thread comes through to the top, the tension is too tight and if the top thread goes through to the bottom, the tension is too loose.

You will need

Sewing machine with darning foot
Machine quilting thread
Two pieces of cotton fabric and one piece of felt, 25.5cm (10in) square
Quilting gloves
Fabric adhesive spray
Scissors

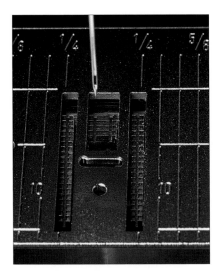

1. Lower the feed dogs by depressing the button on the side of your machine. Refer to your sewing machine manual if this does not seem to be the method on your machine.

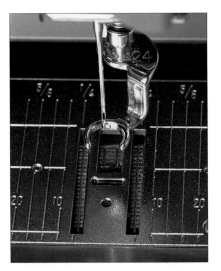

2. Replace your standard foot with the darning foot (or open embroidery foot).

Note
It is a good idea at this time to replace your old needle with a new one – preferably a size 80 Top stitch.

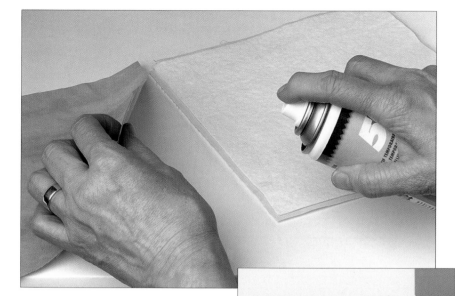

3. Take one piece of fabric and lay it right side down. Place the piece of felt on top and then place the second piece of fabric, right side up on top. Use the spray to keep the fabrics together as 'a quilt sandwich'.

4. Thread the machine quilting thread on to the machine and on to the bobbin and starting in the middle of the 'quilt sandwich', lower the machine needle into the fabric. Raise the needle and this will bring the bobbin thread up to the surface. Holding the two threads to one side, sew one or two small stitches on top of each other to secure them.

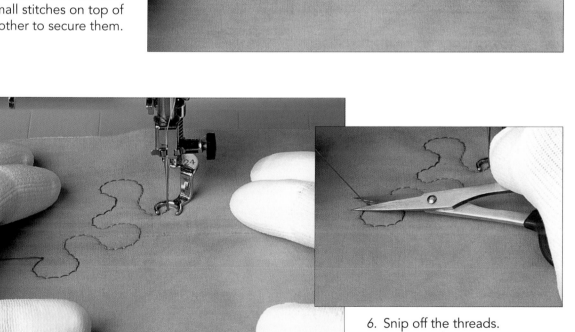

6. Snip off the threads.

5. Wearing quilting gloves, start moving the fabric around to create different shapes.

Free machining patterns

These are all stitches that can be used to fill in a background. It is a good idea to practise these stitches on paper first and once your pencil is flowing on the paper you will be able to do it on fabric as well.

Diagram A

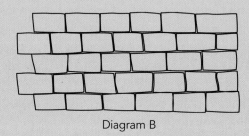

Diagram B

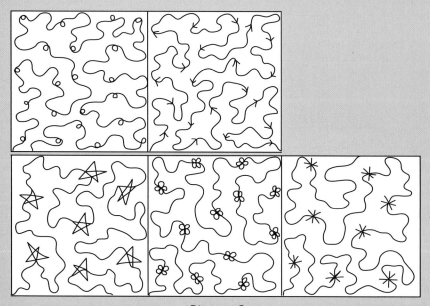

Diagram C

No. 1 This is commonly known as vermicelli or meandering stitch and is the most popular of the filling in stitches.

No. 2 This is a spiral shape. It creates an overall pattern but the same stitch can be used in rows, as can a square version of it (see Diagram A).

No. 3 Circular shapes. These can be boulders or pebbles depending on the size! Good for embroidering paths, beaches etc.

No. 4 Square shapes. Again, you can vary these in size. Large squares cover a surface very quickly. You can elongate the shape and make them into bricks (see Diagram B).

No. 5 This is a wavy line going horizontally and vertically. Very good for filling large spaces very quickly.

No. 6 This particular stitch is very useful for using on skies and water as it flows.

No. 7 This is the vermicelli with an added square every now and then.

No. 8 This is the vermicelli with added twirls and heart shapes. See Diagram C for other vermicelli variations.

23

More free machining patterns

1

This was inspired by the seed head sketches in my sketchbook.

2

This design looks like an ammonite fossil. It is best to draw detailed designs on to the fabric before free machining.

3

These stones can be pebbles or boulders depending on their size and the filling around them, which is a small meandering stitch.

4

Start in the middle of the design and work your way out. Take the stitch out to each corner and to the top, bottom and each side, then fill in the rest.

5

Draw the two squares on to the background fabric then fill them in with meandering stitch. Fill in the rest of the block with straight stitch.

6

Draw the chevron pattern on to the background fabric and then fill in with straight stitch.

7

Lightly draw on the grid pattern and cover with free machining using a narrow zigzag stitch.

10

Go up and down this block in straight stitch taking the stitch out and in to create the shapes.

8

Draw in the middle square and then fill this in with straight stitch. Move the stitching out a little and sew another five or six rows.

9

Use a combination of embroidery stitches on your machine to fill in this block.

Making your own fabric

Making your own background fabric is fun and a variety of effects can be achieved, depending on whether you lay down strips of similar colours or contrasting colours. In this piece I have used different coloured sheer fabrics and a wavy free machine stitch to keep them in place.

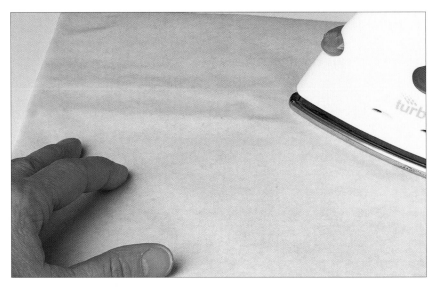

1. Take your piece of felt backing and lay the fusible webbing on top, paper side up. Press the webbing on to the felt, (refer to the manufacturer's instructions) and leave for a minute before peeling off the paper.

2. Tear strips of your sheer fabrics about 3.8cm (1½in) wide and place them on top of the fusible webbing, overlapping them as you go.

3. When you are happy with the result, carefully place a piece of baking parchment on top and then press lightly to keep them in place.

4. Thread your machine with your chosen thread and lower the feed dogs. Start at one side and wearing quilting gloves, stitch a wavy line up and down the piece, keeping the rows fairly close together. Keep changing your machine thread to match the colour of the background strips.

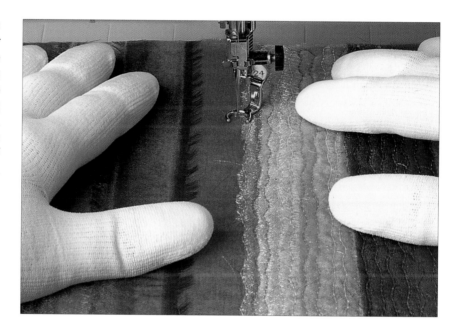

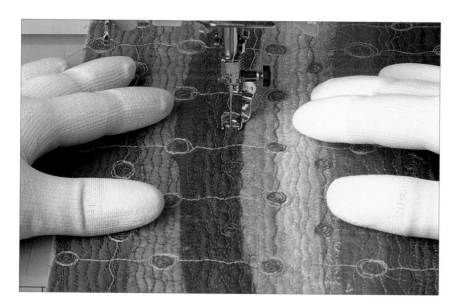

5. Thread the machine with a contrasting thread and start free machining across and up and down the background, adding circles as you go.

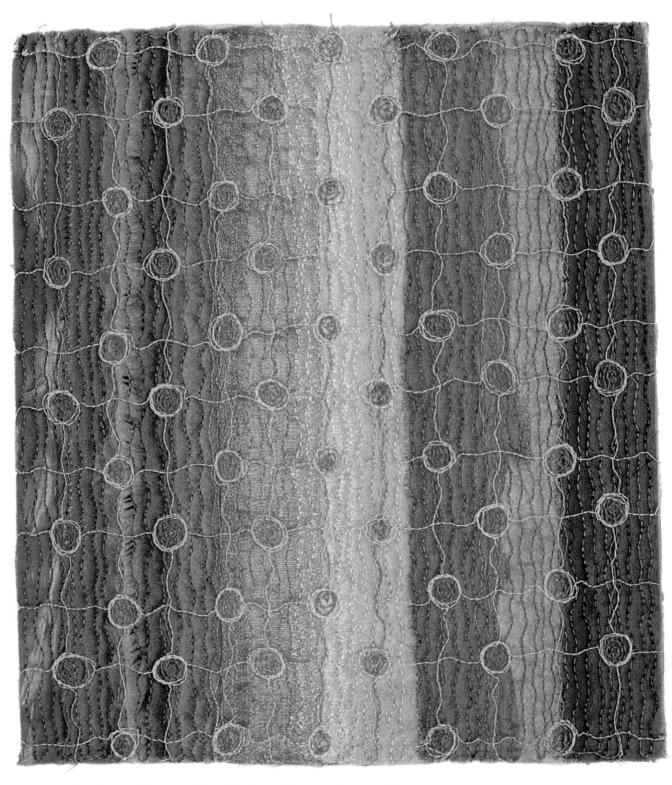

The completed piece of free-machined fabric could be used for any of the bags in this book. You could also try adding thin, torn strips of netting as you free machine and experiment with different quilting stitches.

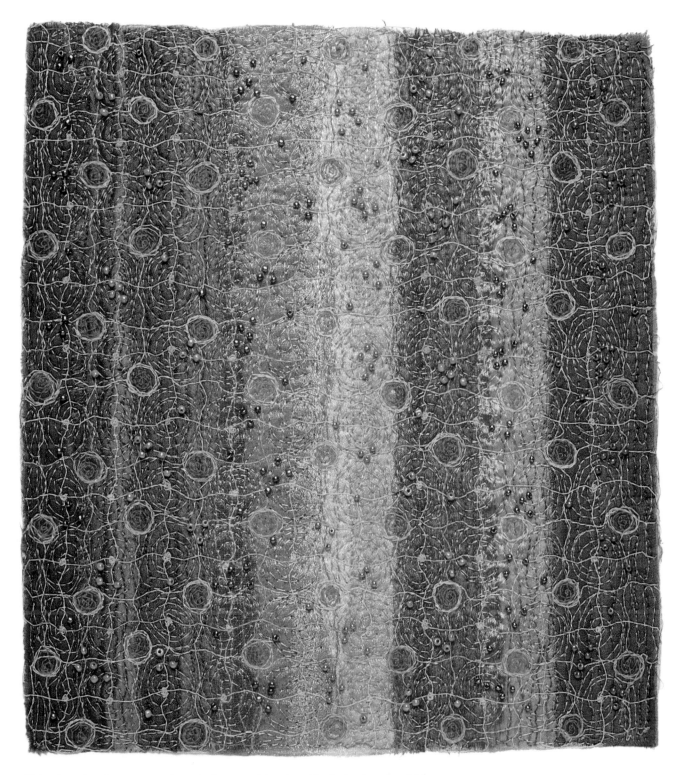

This piece has been more densely free machined and includes beads which were sewn on by hand afterwards. You could sew French knots on to the background to add texture instead of beads.

Weaving strips of fabric together

One of the simplest ways of making a new background is to cut strips of fabric and weave them together. Different effects can be achieved by using only two fabrics and cutting the strips to the same size, or using lots of different fabrics and cutting the strips to different widths. The sample demonstrated here can be made into a much larger piece if you cut a bigger piece of heavyweight interfacing and longer strips.

You will need

Sewing machine with darning foot

Two contrasting fabrics, 12.7 x 12.7cm (5 x 5in)

Variegated machine embroidery thread

Heavyweight interfacing, 12.7 x 12.7cm (5 x 5in)

Fusible webbing, 12.7 x 12.7cm (5 x 5in)

Iron

Pins

Fabric scissors

1. Place the fusible webbing on to the heavyweight interfacing and press it with the iron. When this has cooled down, peel off the backing paper.

2. Cut the two pieces of fabric into 2.5cm (1in) strips and lay them on the interfacing, starting at the top left-hand corner. Secure the strips with pins.

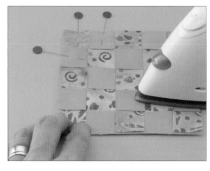

3. When all the strips are in place, press the piece with the iron.

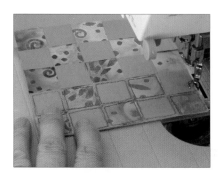

4. Lower the feed dogs on your machine, thread it with the variegated thread and free machine round all the squares, going round each square two or three times.

The finished fabric. I have added washer-shaped beads.

This piece uses more than two fabrics and different width strips. Instead of free machining, a machine embroidery stitch has been used.

This piece has been decorated with rows of stitches very close together.

Using ribbons

Making a background fabric out of ribbons is great fun, and there are such a variety of ribbons in the shops that finding just the colours you need is no problem. Not only haberdashery shops but also florists keep a good supply of ribbons.

You will need

Sewing machine with walking foot
Heavyweight calico for background fabric, 18 x 23cm (7 x 9in)
A selection of ribbons in different widths and colours
Invisible thread
Pins

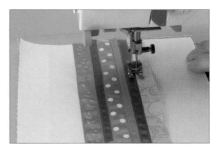

1. Cut a selection of ribbons into 23cm (9in) lengths and, starting in the middle, pin the first ribbon to the background fabric. Sew down each side using invisible thread.

2. Take the next ribbon and pin it down next to the first one. Sew down each side. Continue adding ribbons in this way.

The finished piece.

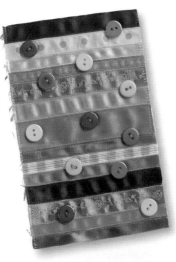

You can embellish ribbon fabric with buttons...

...or beads.

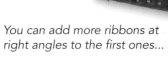

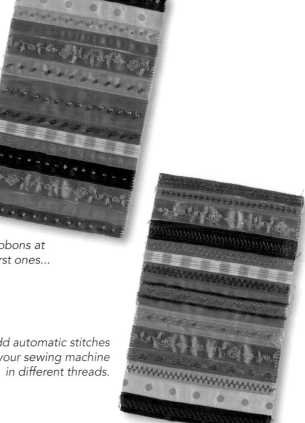

You can add more ribbons at right angles to the first ones...

...or add automatic stitches from your sewing machine in different threads.

Using bondable fibres

Bondable fibres can add a bit of sparkle to your work. There are two types – Hot Fix and Standard. The Hot Fix fibres bond to themselves when placed between baking parchment and pressed with an iron on a silk setting. This makes a sheet of web-like, non-woven fabric. The Standard fibres will not bond to themselves, but a layer can be put between two layers of Hot Fix.

You will need

Selection of Hot Fix bondable fibres
Baking parchment
Iron

1. Take a piece of baking parchment and sprinkle on a selection of fibres.

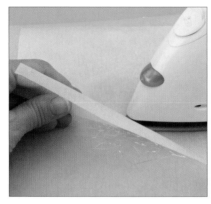

2. Place another sheet of parchment on top. Set the iron to the silk setting. Press. Irons vary in temperature, so if the fibres are not bonding, it may be necessary to increase the temperature slightly.

3. When it has cooled down, remove the fabric.

Note

Changing the iron temperature produces different effects (see below). Always try a test piece first to see what sort of effect you want to achieve.

Fibres pressed with a hot iron – they change to matt.

Fibres pressed with a medium iron – they change colour.

Fibres pressed with a cool iron – they remain sparkly.

Bondable fibres can be used in so many ways but I particularly like using two layers and trapping bits in between.

With snipped ribbons.   With snipped threads.   With small sequins.

Here, two sheets of bondable fibres have been made in different colours, cut into strips and woven together, then pressed again.

Pieces of multicoloured thread have been trapped in between two lots of fibres. Lengths of the thread have then been couched down using an invisible thread.

A sheet of bonded fibres has been cut into petal shapes, sewn round and made up into a flower that could be used to embellish a purse.

Fibres have been bonded on to felt and free machined with a spiral.

33

Making embellishments

There are various techniques you can use to embellish your bags and purses, and here are some ideas.

Quick brooches

  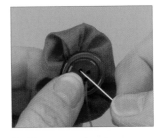 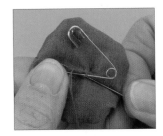

1. Cut out a fabric circle 9cm (3½in) in diameter and with matching thread, make small running stitches close to the edge.

2. Pull the thread tight and make a few stitches to finish off.

3. Sew on a button at the centre of the gathered side.

4. Sew a safety pin on the back.

The finished brooch with some other styles.

Covering a washer with thread

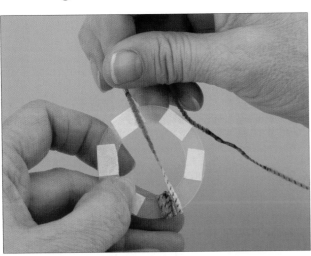

1. Put small pieces of double-sided tape on one side of the washer and peel off the backing. Choose an interesting thread and wind it over the washer until it is covered.

Washers covered in different threads.

Covering a press stud

This technique only works if you use a fine fabric such as silk or lamé.

1. Take a large 15mm (⁵/₈in) press stud and cut two circles of silk 35mm (1³/₈in) in diameter. Place the two circles of silk together and position in between the two sides of the press stud. Press together.

2. Using a thread that matches the silk, sew a running stitch around one of the pieces of silk.

3. Pull the thread to gather the silk circle. Make one or two stitches to secure it.

4. Repeat on the other side of the press stud and put in two stitches to finish off.

The covered press stud. When slip stitching the two halves of the press stud on to a background, sew them on loosely or they will keep popping open.

Making a ribbon bow

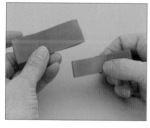   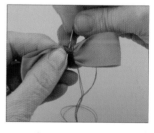

1. Take a length of wide ribbon and fold it as shown, overlapping the ends. Do the same to a shorter length of narrower ribbon.

2. Place the narrower ribbon on top. Measure the middle and put in a pin. Thread a needle and make a few running stitches across the middle of the ribbons.

3. Remove the pin and pull the thread to gather the ribbons.

4. Take a short length of narrow ribbon. Bind it round the middle of the bow and finish off with a few stitches.

The finished ribbon bow with alternative colours.

Making cords

Once you have made your own cords you will never again go out and buy commercial ones as they are great fun to make and will perfectly match your project. You can use fancy threads and an open zigzag stitch so that the threads show through or, if you are covering string, shorten the stitch length to ensure that it is completely covered. When covering string, a useful tip is to use your ordinary threads to cover initially, and then increase the stitch length and do another row in a more decorative thread.

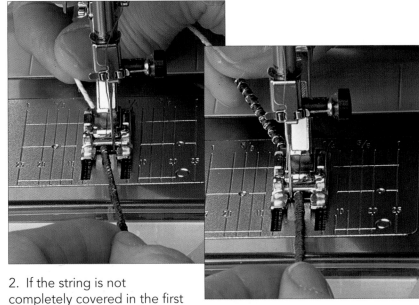

1. Set your sewing machine to the zigzag stitch and fit your appliqué foot. Thread the machine with the same thread on the top and in the bobbin. Take a piece of fine string and place it under the foot, leaving 5cm (2in) behind the foot to hold on to. Set the machine to a zigzag and ensure the stitch is wide enough to cover the string by testing that the needle clears the string on both sides.

2. If the string is not completely covered in the first row, just turn it round and sew over it again.

3. When the string is covered, change your top and bobbin threads to a decorative thread and increase the stitch length. Do one more row to complete the cord.

Note
You can use a cording foot if you have one or lower the feed dogs and use a darning foot. I like the appliqué foot because I can see what I am doing.

Opposite
The finished cord (from bottom left) with a variety of cords in different colours. If you put three cords side by side, you can sew them together with a zigzag stitch to make a wider cord or plait them together to make a chunkier cord.

Petal Bag

This tasselled little bag is very easily made from two folded circles and a lot of free machining. It reminds me of a flower gradually opening up and the petals unfurling.

You will need

Sewing machine with darning foot

Quarter metre (10in) fabric for the outside of the bag

Quarter metre (10in) felt

Quarter metre (10in) lining fabric

Plate 16.5cm (6 ½in) in diameter

Fabric adhesive spray

Twelve lengths of a variety of textured and decorative threads 127cm (50in) long for the handle and five lengths 150cm (60in) long for the tassel

Tiny beads

Two small washers

Machine quilting thread

Small piece of mounting card, cutting mat and craft knife

PVA glue and spatula

Fine marker

Scissors and pins

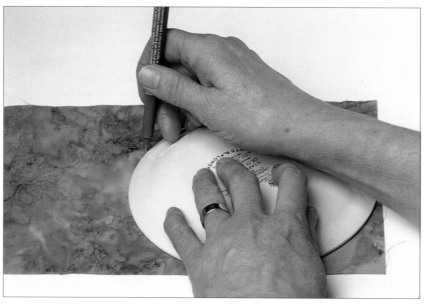

1. Take your main piece of fabric and cut out a piece 17.7 x 35.5cm (7 x 14in). On the right side draw two circles with a fine marker, using the plate as a template.

Note

A quarter metre (10in) assumes that the fabric or felt is 112cm (44in) wide, so that your piece will measure 25 x 112cm (10 x 44in).

2. Take the piece of felt and cut out a piece 17.7 x 35.5cm (7 x 14in). Spray with the fabric adhesive spray. Place the fabric on top.

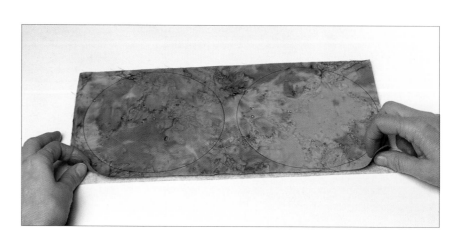

3. Thread the machine with machine quilting thread, lower the feed dogs and attach the darning foot. Fill the marked shapes with free machine circles. When complete, sew round the edge on the drawn line.

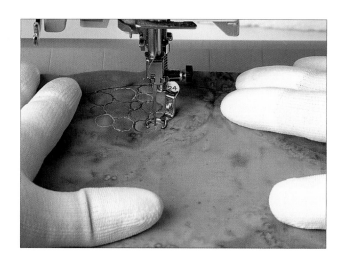

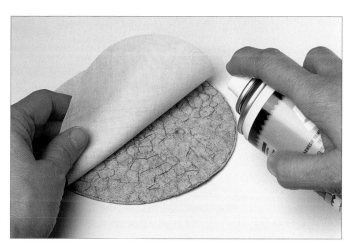

4. Carefully cut out the circles just outside the sewn line and sew tiny beads at random all over their surface.

5. Take your lining fabric and cut out a piece 17.7 x 35.5cm (7 x 14in). Draw round the plate twice and cut out the circles. Place your machined and beaded circles right side down and spray the backs with glue. Position the lining circles on top. They may be slightly larger as the fabric shrinks when quilted, so you may need to trim a small amount of lining from the edge of each circle.

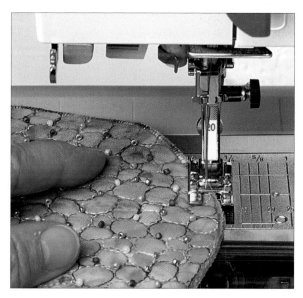

6. Put the machine back to normal sewing and attach an appliqué foot. Set the stitch to zigzag and sew round the edge of each lined circle. You might have to do this twice to cover the edges.

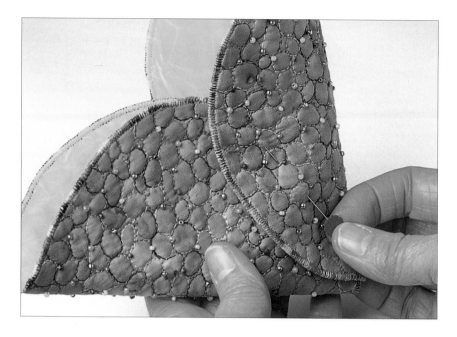

7. Fold the circular petals in half to get the shape of the bag and secure with pins.

8. Put tiny dabs of PVA glue on the underside of each petal and place a heavy book on top of the bag until the glue dries.

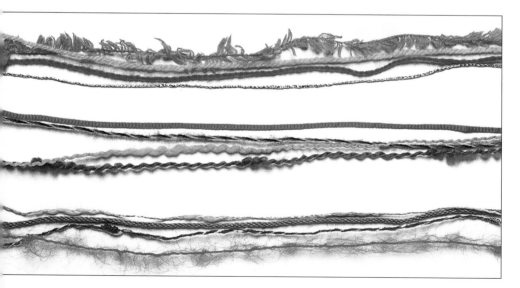

9. Take the twelve decorative, textured threads 127cm (50in) long. Divide them into three groups of four. Take one group and cover it with zigzag stitch, as when making a cord. Make the zigzag stitch very wide and the stitch length very long so that the threads show through.
Repeat with the other groups of thread to make three cords.

10. Anchor the three zigzagged cords; here they are pinned to a basket. Plait them together.

11. Feed the plaited threads through a washer for about 2.5cm (1in) and fold back the end.

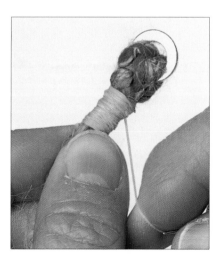

12. Thread a needle with a matching thread and wrap the loose ends. Repeat the other end.

13. Using the same thread, sew the washers by hand on to each side of the bag.

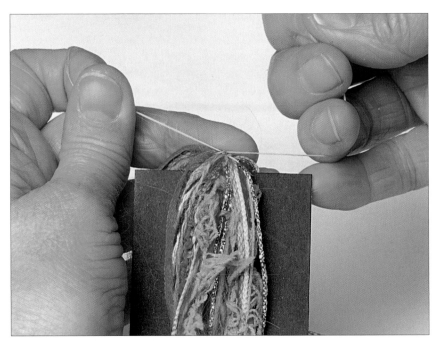

14. To make the tassel, cut a piece of mounting card, 11.5 x 5cm (4½ x 2in). Take your five threads, hold them at the bottom of the card and wrap them round several times.

15. Thread a needle with a long length of the same thread as you used in step 12 and tie at the top.

16. Cut the threads at the bottom of the card.

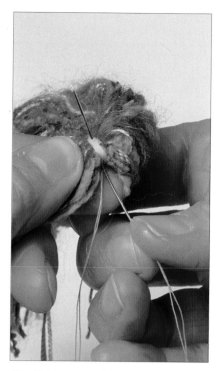

17. Taking the threaded needle, wrap the yellow thread round the top of the tassel where you tied it. Then take the needle up through the top of the tassel.

18. Using the same yellow thread, bind round the collar of the tassel.

19. To tie off, push the needle back down through the tassel and cut the thread.

20. Use dressmaking scissors to trim the bottom of the tassel.

21. Sew the tassel on to the bottom of the bag using the same yellow thread.

The finished Petal Bag.

In this version, decorative threads have been knotted at intervals for the handle.

French knots could be added instead of beads and smaller versions of the bag could be made by varying the size of the original circle.

Mezzaluna Bag

I had the idea for this bag when I was chopping herbs one day. I was using a mezzaluna, which is a piece of kitchen equipment with a curved blade and a handle on each side. Mezzaluna means 'half moon' in Italian.

You will need

Sewing machine with a darning foot and an appliqué or cording foot

Quarter metre (10in) of three different coloured cotton fabrics

Quarter metre (10in) of felt

Quarter metre (10in) of fusible webbing

Various threads to match

Decorative threads for couching

Invisible thread

Length of tubing, 30.5cm (12in)

Beads small enough to thread through the tubing

Length of wire, 40.5cm (16in), thin enough to thread the beads on to

Tiny beads

Fabric glue stick

Fabric adhesive spray

Baking parchment and iron

Quilting gloves

Fine marker

Large needle

Pins

Note
A quarter metre (10in) assumes that the fabric or felt is 112cm (44in) wide, so that your piece will measure 25 x 112cm (10 x 44in).

Patterns for the front and back and for the base of the bag, printed half size. Enlarge them to double the size on a photocopier, trace them, stick the tracings on to thicker paper and cut the templates out. Mark the position of the dots.

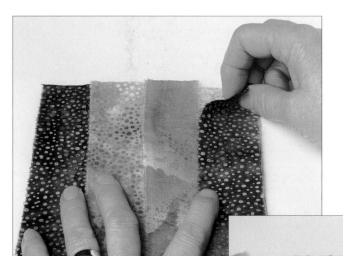

1. Cut a piece of felt and a piece of fusible webbing, each 20.3 x 47cm (8 x 18½in). Press the webbing on to the felt and peel off the backing paper. Tear the three different colours of cotton fabric into strips about 4cm (1½in) wide. Cut the strips into 20.3cm (8in) lengths and place them on top of the fusible webbing, overlapping slightly so that the background does not show.

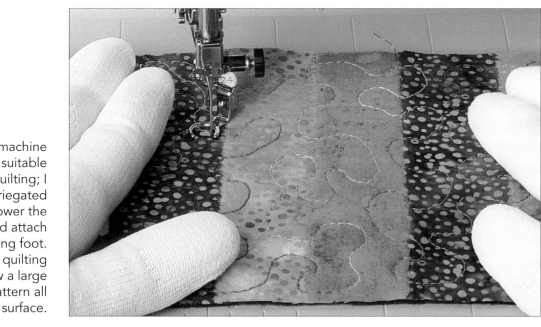

2. Place a piece of baking parchment on top and press with an iron.

3. Set up your machine with thread suitable for machine quilting; I have used a variegated thread here. Lower the feed dogs and attach your darning foot. Wearing your quilting gloves, sew a large vermicelli pattern all over the surface.

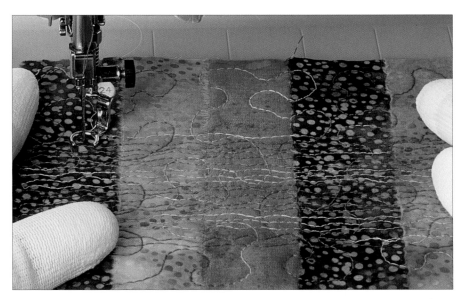

4. Sew across the strips of fabric with a wavy stitch, keeping the lines of stitching quite close together.

5. Take your decorative threads and couch them on to the background. Use an invisible thread on top and an ordinary thread in the bobbin. Set your machine to zigzag wide enough to cover the threads that you are couching.

Note
To couch threads you can either use an appliqué foot or a cording foot. The cording foot has a groove underneath it that lets thicker threads go through more easily. I prefer to use an appliqué foot as I can see what I am doing.

6. Choose one of the fabrics for the base and cut a piece approximately 10 x 28cm (4 x 11in). Also cut a piece of felt the same size. Using the fabric adhesive spray, bond the fabric and felt. To quilt the base, put a thicker thread on the bobbin and an invisible thread on the top of the machine. Lower the feed dogs and attach the darning foot. Place the base of the bag felt side up under the needle and free machine circles over the entire surface.

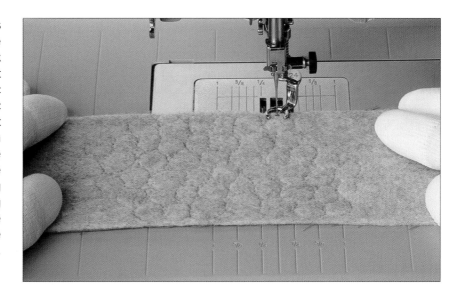

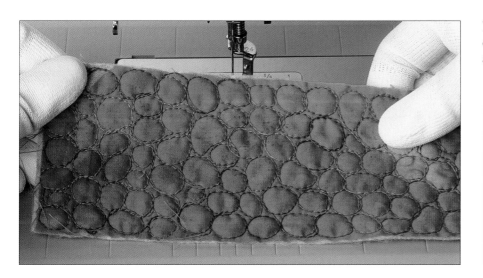

7. When you turn the base over, the thicker thread will appear on the right side.

Note
This method works well with any thread that does not sew easily when threaded on the top, such as thick threads and some metallic threads.

8. For the lining, choose one of your fabrics and draw and cut out a front, back and base using the templates and a fine marker.

9. With right sides together, pin the lining base to the lining front, matching the dots. Change your machine to normal sewing and sew between the dots, removing pins as you go. Do the same with the lining back.

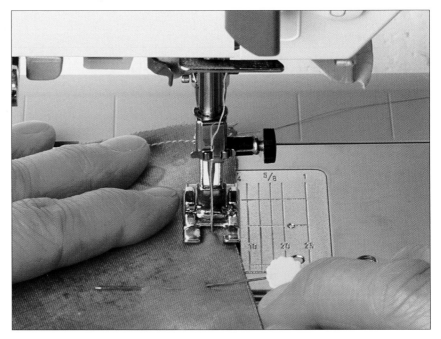

10. Sew the side seams of the lining from the dots to the top edge.

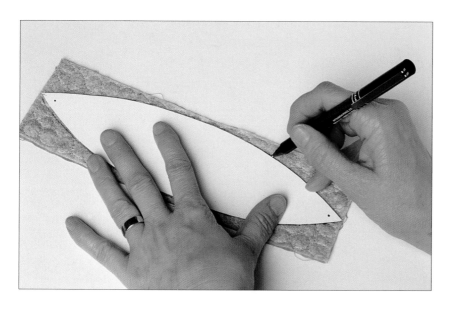

11. Position the front and back templates on the reverse of the couched fabric as in the diagram below. Position the base template on the reverse of the quilted base fabric. Draw around the templates with a fine marker, marking the dots as before.

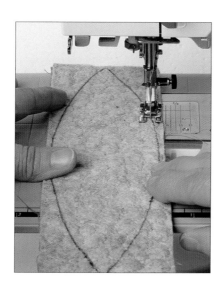

12. Sew along all the drawn lines to ensure that the couching and stitching does not unravel. Cut out just outside the line. Keep the remnants of the couched fabric – they will be used later.

13. Stitch the base to the front and back in the same way as you did with the lining.

14. Turn the bag right side out. Place the lining in the bag and tack around the top edge. Thread up your machine with a matching thread on the top and in the bobbin and change to a zigzag stitch. Sew around the top edge until covered.

15. To make the handle, thread the wire through the tubing and bend it over at one end to ensure the beads stay in place. Start threading your beads on to the other end of the wire until you have filled the whole tube. Bend the wire over at the other end.

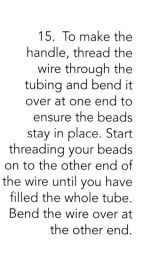

16. To attach the handle to the bag, take a large needle and make a hole at the top of the side seam. Remove the needle and thread one end of the wire through the hole. Bend upwards and wind round the base of the tubing. Make a corresponding hole on the other side of the bag, unravel the other end of the wire and secure in the same way.

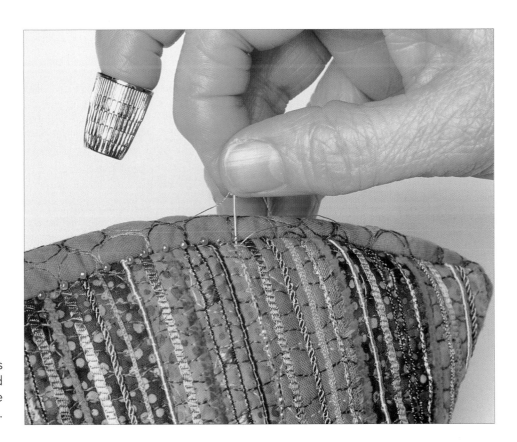

17. Sew tiny beads down each side, around the base and around the top of the bag.

The finished Mezzaluna Bag. To make the tag, draw a heart shape on the remnants of the bag fabric. Sew a line round the drawn line and cut out the shape just outside this line. Repeat to make another heart. Take a thick thread or cord about 20.3cm (8in) long and wrap it with two rows of zigzags. Place the hearts wrong sides together. Fold the cord and place the ends in between the top of the hearts. Secure with a little fabric glue. Sew round the edge of the hearts with a zigzag stitch.

The size of the bag could be altered by enlarging or reducing the pattern. You can also make tags in different shapes.

Boxy Bag

I used to love my grandmother's knitting bag which had wooden handles, and thought I would make an updated version, although rather smaller.

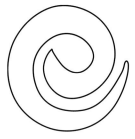

The pattern for the spiral, shown full size. Transfer it on to card and cut it out to make a template.

You will need

Sewing machine with darning foot and appliqué foot

Quarter metre (10in) of light fabric

Quarter metre (10in) of dark fabric

Quarter metre (10in) of fusible webbing

Quarter metre (10in) of felt

25cm (10in) heavyweight interfacing

Threads to match fabrics

¾ metre (30in) ribbon

Fabric glue stick

Invisible thread

Two pieces of dowelling, each 23cm (9in) long

Acrylic paint and brush

PVA glue

Iron

Needle

Scissors

Note

A quarter metre (10in) assumes that the fabric or felt is 112cm (44in) wide, so that your piece will measure 25 x 112cm (10 x 44in).

1. Cut six strips, 15.2 x 5cm (6 x 2in) in the dark fabric and six strips in the light fabric. For the front, lay five strips side by side, alternating the colours. Make an identical set for the back. The remaining two pieces will be the sides. For the base of the bag cut one piece 19 x 5cm (7½ x 2in).

2. Sew the five strips for the bag front together with a 6mm (¼in) seam allowance and press the seams open.

3. Cut 6mm (¼in) off each side so that each piece measures 19 x 15.2cm (7½ x 6in).

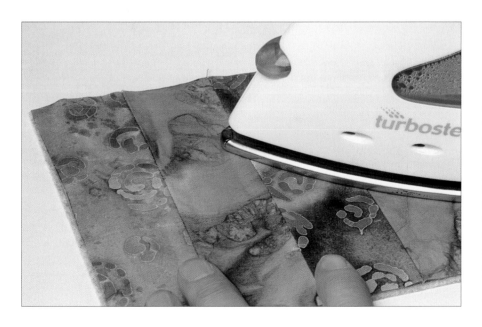

4. Take the felt and the fusible webbing and out of each of these cut two pieces 19 x 15.2cm (7½ x 6in), two pieces 15.2 x 5cm (6 x 2in) and one piece 19 x 5cm (7½ x 2in). Place the fusible webbing on to the back of the bag front and press. Peel off the backing and then press on to the piece of felt. Do this also to the bag back, the two sides and the base.

5. Cut two strips of fabric, one in dark, the other in light, 2.5 x 30.5cm (1 x 12in). Sew these together and press the seam open.

6. Cut a piece of fusible webbing 3.8 x 30.5cm (1½ x 12in) and press it on to the back of the strip. Take the spiral template and use a fine marker to draw around it eight times along the length of the strip. Cut out the shapes and peel off the backing.

7. Place four spirals on the front of the bag and four on the back, positioning them so that the colours reverse and the seam lines line up with the seam lines on the bag. Press.

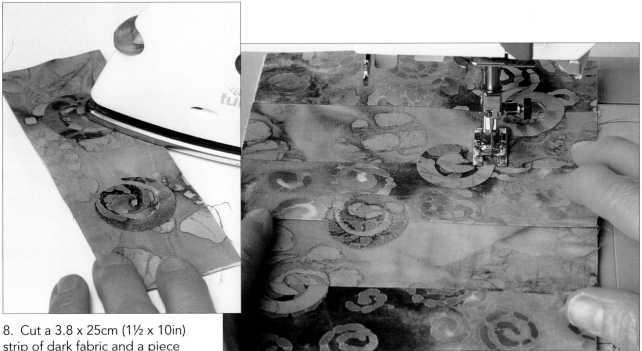

8. Cut a 3.8 x 25cm (1½ x 10in) strip of dark fabric and a piece of fusible webbing the same size and bond them together. Using the same spiral template, cut out seven spirals and bond two on each of the side pieces and three on the base.

9. Set your machine to a zigzag stitch and using invisible thread, sew round the outside of these shapes with a small open stitch. Do this on the front, the back, both sides and the base.

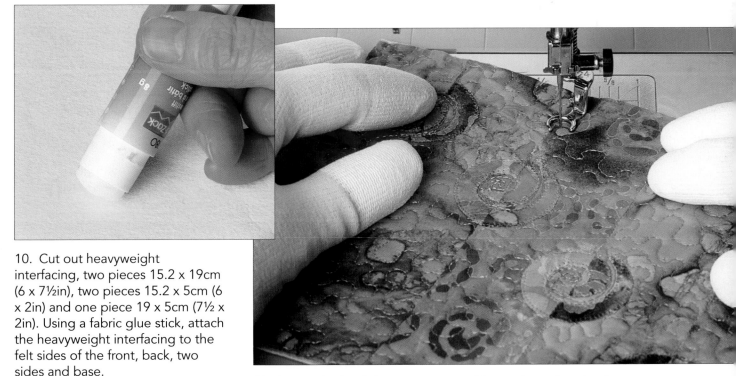

10. Cut out heavyweight interfacing, two pieces 15.2 x 19cm (6 x 7½in), two pieces 15.2 x 5cm (6 x 2in) and one piece 19 x 5cm (7½ x 2in). Using a fabric glue stick, attach the heavyweight interfacing to the felt sides of the front, back, two sides and base.

11. Lower the feed dogs on your machine and attach a darning foot. Using threads to match your fabrics, free machine a vermicelli stitch over the surfaces of all five pieces. Trim the edges if necessary.

12. For the lining, take one of your fabrics and cut two pieces 15.2 x 19cm (6 x 7½in), two pieces 15.2 x 5cm (6 x 2in) and one piece 19 x 5cm (7½ x 2in). Use the fabric glue stick on the back of the heavyweight interfacing and stick it on to the lining pieces.

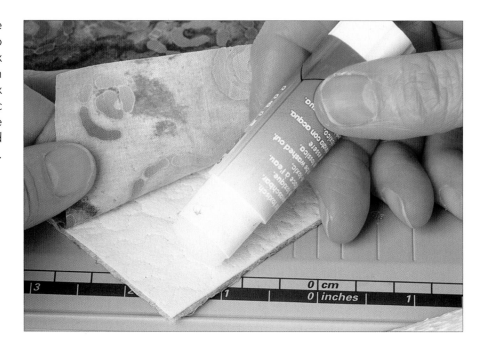

13. Change your machine back to normal stitching and attach the appliqué foot. Set to a medium width zigzag stitch and sew round the edges of all pieces with a matching thread. Depending on how closely you stitch, you might have to go round the edges once or twice to cover.

14. For the tags, cut four pieces of heavyweight interfacing, 3.2 x 11.5cm (1¼ x 4½in) and four pieces of the dark fabric 3 x 13.3cm (3½ x 5¼). Fold the fabric over the interfacing as shown, apply fabric glue stick to keep it in place, and press it. Change your machine back to free machining and sew a vermicelli stitch all over the tags.

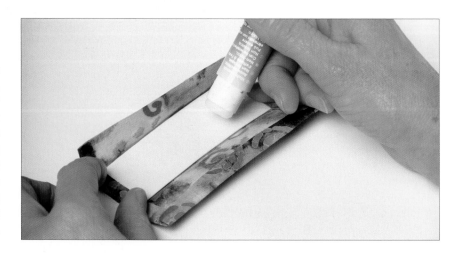

15. Place the tag in line with the first seam, leaving the zigzagged edge clear, and secure it with a pin. Fold the tag down to the inside of the bag to form a loop. Using thread to match the tag, secure the tag firmly to the bag. Repeat with the other tags, placing one in each corner of the bag, front and back.

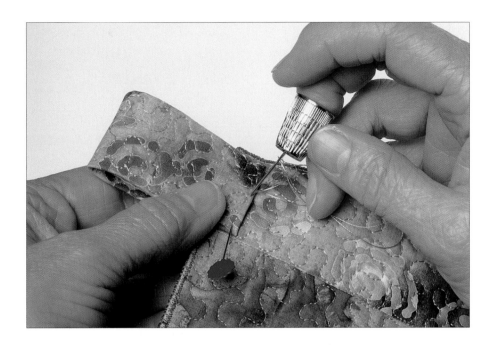

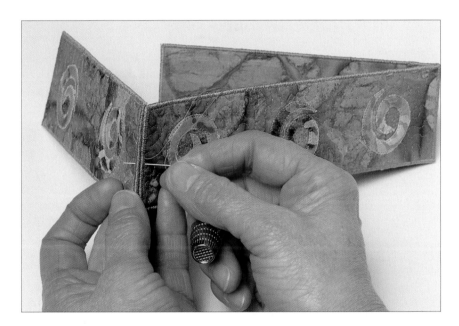

16. Use ladder stitch and invisible thread to hand stitch the two sides of the bag and the base together.

17. Sew this strip to the front of the bag and then sew it to the back.

18. Take your lengths of dowelling, paint them with acrylic paint and allow them to dry. Put a little PVA glue inside the top of each tag and slip the dowelling inside. Put a peg on each side of each tag to keep the dowelling handles secure and leave for an hour to dry.

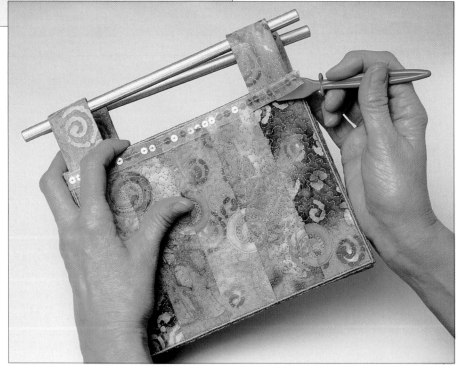

19. Attach the ribbon to the top of the bag with tiny dabs of PVA glue.

The finished Boxy Bag.

*Appliqué was added to these bags, together
with beads and ribbon.*

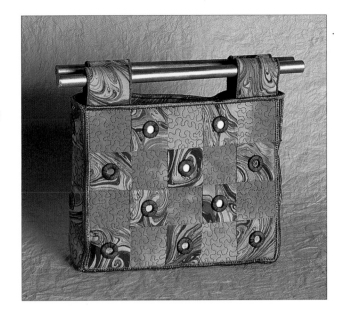

This bag has a checkerboard pattern and covered washers over shisha mirrors.

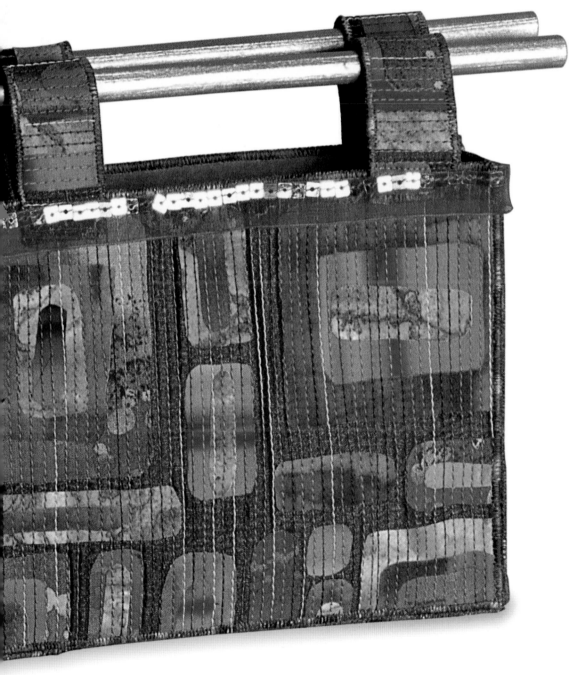

Bangles Bag

This bag was inspired by a shop selling an abundance of pretty accessories including brightly coloured plastic bangles in various different shapes. The bangles seemed ideal for use as handles, and could be chosen to complement the fabric and threads used, as well as the shape of the bag.

You will need

Sewing machine with walking foot, darning foot and appliqué foot

Quarter metre (10in) of main fabric

Quarter metre (10in) of felt

Quarter metre (10in) of lining fabric

Variety of metallic threads

Beads

Two bangles

Mounting card, craft knife and cutting mat

Rotary cutting or ordinary ruler

PVA glue and spatula

Fabric adhesive spray

Fabric glue stick

Small piece of heavyweight interfacing

Pins

Weights

Needle

Iron

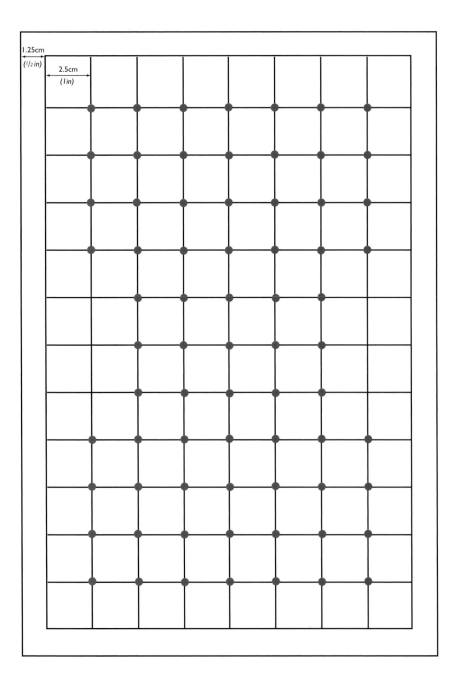

1.25cm
(1/2 in)

2.5cm
(1in)

Note
A quarter metre (10in) assumes that the fabric or felt is 112cm (44in) wide, so that your piece will measure 25 x 112cm (10 x 44in).

The pattern for the grid, printed half size. The pattern also shows where the beads should go.

1. Take your main fabric and cut out a piece 33 x 23cm (13 x 9in). Using a fine marker, draw the grid lines on the fabric as shown on the pattern opposite. I find that using a rotary cutting ruler like the one shown is helpful as it has a grid printed on it and you can see through it, but you could use an ordinary ruler.

2. Take your felt and cut out a piece 33 x 23cm (13 x 9in). Spray with the fabric adhesive spray and place your fabric on top, grid side up.

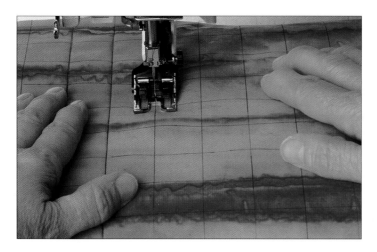

3. Set your machine to normal sewing and if you have one, attach a walking foot. Sew along all the grid lines with a metallic thread on top and a normal sewing thread in a matching colour underneath.

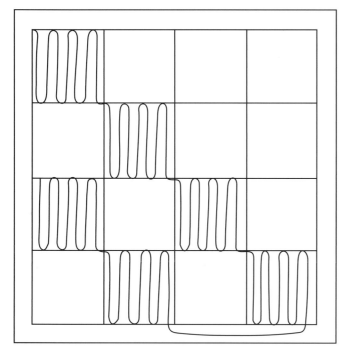

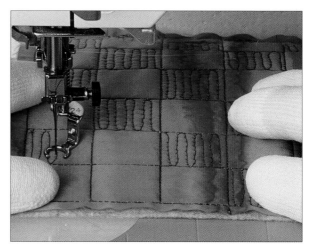

4. Lower the feed dogs, attach the darning foot and start sewing up and down in alternate squares. This can be a continuous process, working diagonally across the grid as shown in the diagram on the left.

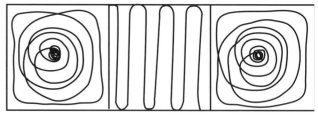

5. In the remaining squares, start in the middle and sew in a spiral towards the edge, then come back in again and finish off with two or three stitches in the middle, as shown in the diagram on the right.

6. Sew on the beads as shown in the pattern on page 68, leaving spaces for sewing up the bag.

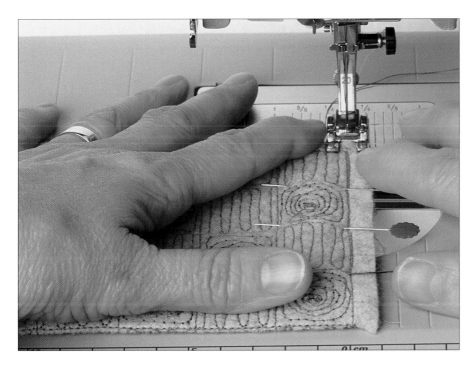

7. Fold the bag right sides together and pin along the edges, aligning the grid lines. Sew along each side and trim the edges down to 6mm (¼in).

8. Fold back the bottom corner edge and measure 5cm (2in). You will be able to see on the reverse where your stitching is. Pin and then stitch across. Do the same to the other corner edge.

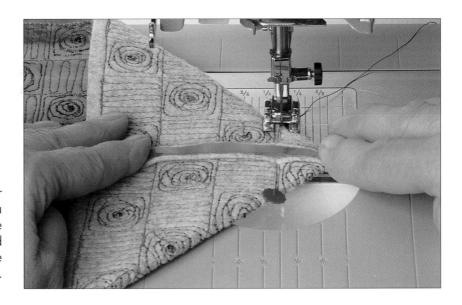

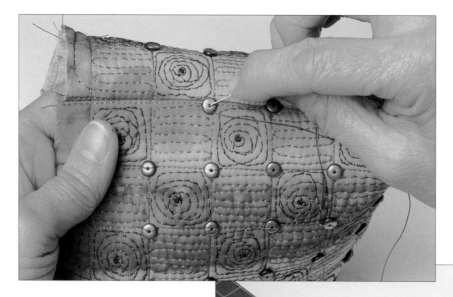

9. Carefully turn the bag right sides out to make sure you have sewn evenly and then press the seams open. Sew the remaining beads along the two edges and at the bottom. Leave the top until later.

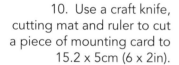

10. Use a craft knife, cutting mat and ruler to cut a piece of mounting card to 15.2 x 5cm (6 x 2in).

11. Put dabs of glue on the base of the bag and put the mounting card on top. Place weights in the bag and leave for an hour.

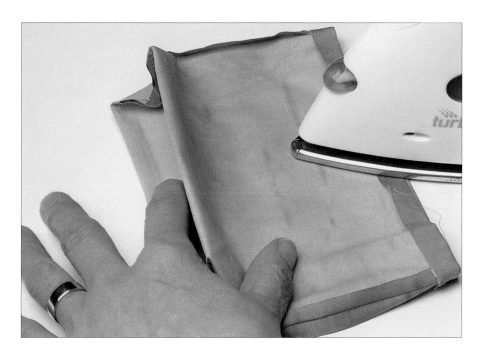

12. Sew the lining in the same way as the bag including the corner edges. Cut off the excess and press the seams open. Fold over the top edge 1.3cm (½in) and press.

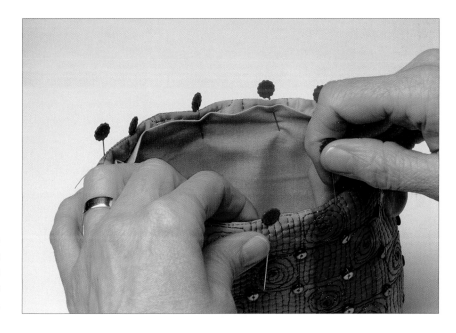

13. Place the lining inside the bag. Fold over the 1.3cm (½in) seam allowance at the top of the bag and pin the lining and bag together.

14. For the tags holding down the bangles, cut two pieces of heavyweight inferfacing 1.3 x 10cm (½ x 4in) and two pieces of the main fabric 4.4 x 10cm (1¾ x 4in). Place the interfacing on top of the fabric. Apply fabric glue stick to the interfacing and fold over. Press with an iron.

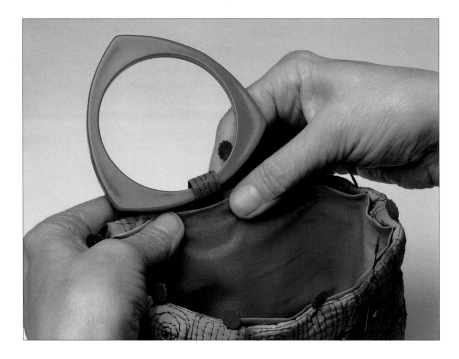

15. With metallic thread, sew up and down the tags and then fold them over each of the bangles and insert the ends in the centre of each side as close as possible to the bag. Tack all the way round.

16. Using metallic thread, sew as close to the top of the bag as possible to secure it.

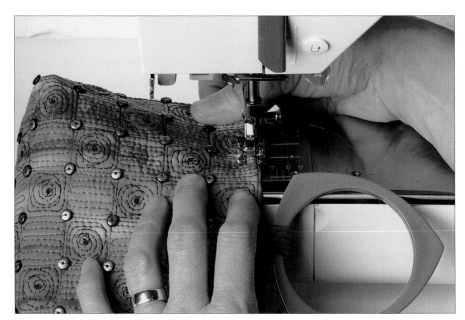

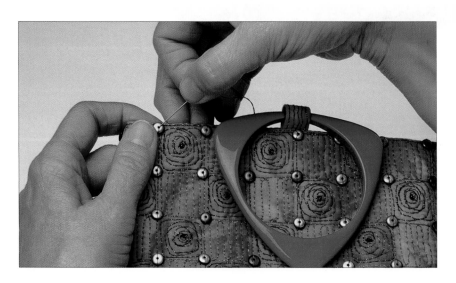

17. Sew beads along the top row of the bag to finish it.

The basic shape for this bag can be varied to make it wider or taller. It can be made with fabric you have made yourself or with crazy patchwork.

Crazy Patchwork Bag

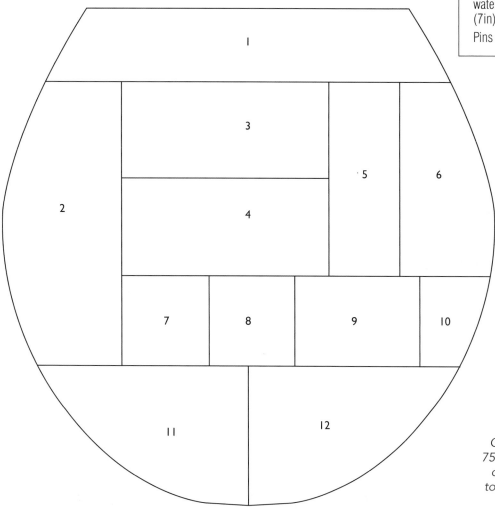

The lovely thing about crazy patchwork is that you can use different weights of fabric as they are laid onto a background piece and then sewn down. It is a nice idea to take pieces of fabric or beads that mean something to you, such as fabric left over from making a child's dress or buttons and beads from your mother's button box, and incorporate these into the finished item. This particular bag was inspired by a beautiful bouquet of flowers I was given, all purples and greens.

You will need

Sewing machine with darning foot and appliqué foot

Selection of fabrics: silk, lamé, velvet, cotton

Threads to match

Fusible webbing, 23 x 40.7cm (9 x 16in)

Felt, 23 x 40.7cm (9 x 16in)

Baking parchment and iron

Beads

Four 1.5cm ($^5/_8$ in) washers

Double-sided tape and PVA glue

43cm (17in) length of medium gauge wire and larger beads for the handle

Various variegated and metallic threads for machine embroidery

25.4cm (10in) square piece of water soluble film and a 17.8cm (7in) embroidery hoop

Pins

The pattern for the Crazy Patchwork Bag, shown at 75 per cent of full size. Enlarge it on a photocopier, transfer it on to card and cut the shape out to make a template.

1. Use the template to cut out two pieces of fusible webbing. Place them on top of the felt and press with an iron. Cut round the shapes and peel off the backing paper.

2. Transfer the full size pattern on to thin paper and number each piece. Cut out the pieces.

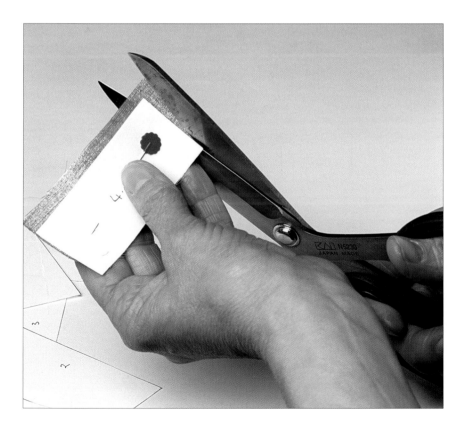

3. Take the paper pieces and pin them on to your chosen fabrics. Cut round each piece twice, making one set for the front and one set for the back.

5. Place on an ironing board and put a piece of baking parchment on top. Press very gently without moving the iron backwards and forwards to prevent the pieces from moving.

4. Lay each piece of fabric on your background felt, fusible webbing right side up, following the numbering. Make sure no background is showing.

6. Set up the sewing machine for normal sewing. Use a variegated thread and do a trial piece: choose three or four of the standard stitches on your sewing machine, suitable for covering the raw edges. You can use just a satin stitch if you wish. Start to sew along the joins between fabric pieces, beginning with the line between pieces 3 and 4. Then sew all the vertical lines, and finish off by sewing the horizontal lines.

7. Now is your chance to embellish the background fabric pieces. Do some free machining in different patterns. To make the star pattern, start in the middle and sew round and round to make a circle. Then take the needle up as if to twelve o'clock and add a little circle. Sew back down to the bottom of the central circle, then sew down to six o'clock and add another little circle. Repeat at three o'clock and nine o'clock. Now fill in all the other points on the clock in the same way, so that you have a twelve-pointed star.

8. Add beads, but do not sew them too close to the edge seam allowance. Repeat steps 4 to 8 to make the back of the bag.

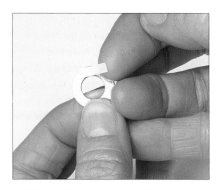

9. To make your own shisha mirrors, attach a small amount of double-sided tape to the back of a washer and peel off the backing. This will secure the thread as you start wrapping.

10. Cut lengths of three different threads, thread them all through a needle and knot the ends together. Tie on to the washer, on top of the sticky tape, and wrap the thread round and round the washer until it is covered. Secure the end.

11. Place the covered washer on top of a piece of shisha glass or a large sequin and secure with PVA glue. Then glue it on to your background fabric and put it aside until it is completely dry.

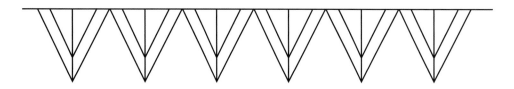

The pattern for the lacy border, shown full size.

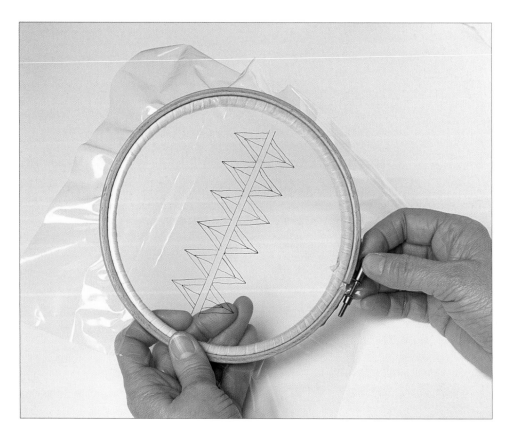

12. To make your lacy border, take your water soluble film and trace off the pattern shown above twice, as shown in the photograph. Secure the water soluble film in your embroidery hoop.

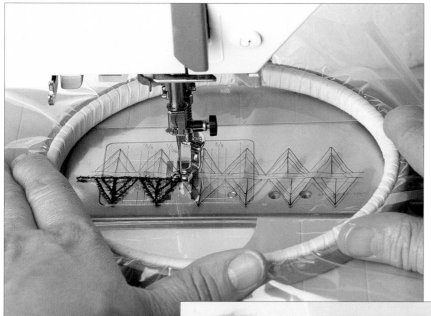

13. Set your sewing machine to free machining, lower the feed dogs and attach the darning foot. With metallic thread on top and in the bobbin, sew over the pattern, linking up all the stitches in each border. Follow the manufacturer's instructions to dissolve the water soluble film and allow the two borders to dry. Sew a bead on to the bottom of each triangle as shown.

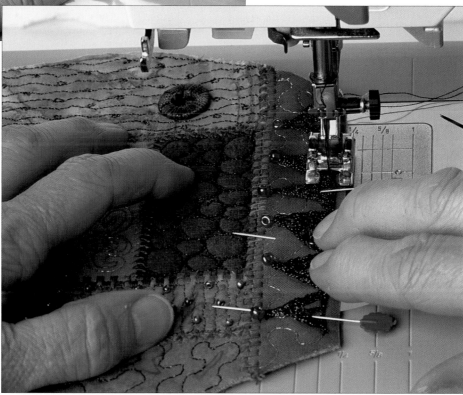

14. Place a lacy border 3mm (1/8 in) from the top of the bag. Set the machine for normal sewing and secure the top of the border with a straight stitch. Repeat with the other border on the back of the bag.

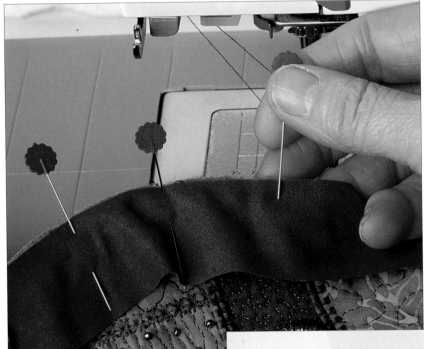

15. Take one of your fabrics and cut a 3.2 x 45.7cm (1¼ x 18in) strip. Pin it, right sides together round the edges of the front piece.

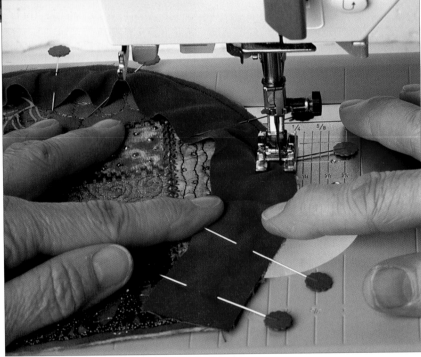

16. Change to normal thread and sew round with a 6mm (¼in) seam allowance. Attach the back piece in the same way so that the strip forms a gusset. Turn the bag right sides out.

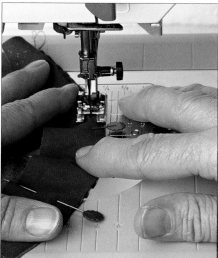

17. Using the original template, cut out front and back pieces of lining and a 3.2 x 45.7cm (1¼ x 18in) strip for a gusset. Sew them together in the same way as the bag.

18. Place the lining inside the bag and pin it round the top. Sew a row of straight stitches round the top, then trim.

19. Change the machine to zigzag stitch and with metallic thread on the top and in the bobbin, sew round the top to neaten the edge.

20. Take your piece of wire and thread it with the beads.

21. Attach the beaded wire handle by making a hole in the side of the bag with a large needle, and then threading the wire through the hole and wrapping round to finish off. Do the same to the other side.

The finished Crazy Patchwork Bag.

You could make your own crazy patterns or use different shaped pieces to bond to the background. You could also cover the seams by sewing ribbons over them or couching thicker threads.

PURSES

Ever since I was a child I have liked containers, whether they were boxes, bags or purses. I think this is a natural instinct in girls and women, to gather, collect, organise and keep safe special items.

My grandparents lived by the sea and they had a beach hut. I used to love nothing more than collecting shells, interesting stones and general flotsam and jetsam from the beach and storing them away in the beach hut. I would use old shoe boxes, any tin that had a lid or even empty matchboxes if the shells were small enough.

When I learned to sew as a child, special fabrics such as silk and velvet were precious, so any bits left over from my mother's and grandmother's dressmaking were carefully stored away in my own sewing box. I remember having a small purse that my mother had embroidered, in which I kept special buttons. I still have some of the buttons, but alas the embroidered purse is long gone.

I suppose it was only a matter of time before I started making my own purses, and there is a great satisfaction in making a purse that reflects the uniqueness and individuality of the creator.

There are times when all you need is a purse rather than a larger bag. It just needs to hold today's essentials such as a credit card, phone and lipstick. As purses need to be secure, I have used zips and magnetic clasps to keep the contents safe.

The purses can be fun, they can be sensible, they can be sophisticated and they can reflect your own personality – this can be done by simply adding a bow or a buckle. Most of all they must be enjoyed.

Planning a purse

Getting started on a new project is very exciting. Having decided to start on a project from my Indian scrapbook (see page 16–17), I went through my fabrics to decide which ones to use. I thought silks and lamés were perfect for this purse and the colour palette I wanted to use was bright jewel colours so I picked out the warm and rich colours shown here.

I did the same with my threads, using rayons and metallics. I tend to keep my threads in baskets, sorted into warm, cool or neutral colours. For this project I chose only from the warm and cool selections.

I also picked out embellishments such as velvet ribbons, sequins, beads, sari yarn, shells and shisha glass. You might not end up using all the embellishments you pick out at the beginning of a project, but it is good to have a choice.

This is the fabric I made for the Indian Purse (see pages 94–99). It is decorated with free machine embroidery, beads and sequins, and edged with sari yarn.

Indian Purse

Please read all the instructions before starting any of the projects. Note that a 6mm (¼in) seam is used throughout unless otherwise stated.

This purse is inspired by all the beautiful colours found in Indian textiles, colours that you would perhaps not normally put together but which work well in an 'over the top' sort of way!

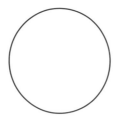

The template for the circle design.

1. Take the top fabric and with the marking pencil draw lines down the length of the fabric measuring from the left-hand side as follows: 5cm (2in); 3.2cm (1¼in); 3.8cm (1½in); 3.2cm (1¼in) and 5cm (2in).

2. Take the fusible webbing and trace six circles from the template, then draw twelve 2.5cm (1in) squares. Draw four 3.8cm (1½in) squares with a diagonal line across each.

3. Cut the fusible webbing into the separate sections as shown and place on top of each of the contrasting fabrics. Press with the iron.

4. Cut out each shape, peel off the paper backing and place the shapes on the top fabric as shown. When you are satisfied that they are in the correct positions, press with the iron.

5. Place the top fabric on top of the wadding and place the thin cotton underneath. Spray the layers with fabric adhesive to keep them in place.

6. Set up your machine for free machining by lowering the feed dogs and putting on a darning foot. Choose a thread that matches the circles in the middle and start by sewing round and round each circle in a spiral shape.

7. Continue sewing round each shape, changing threads where necessary. Finish off by couching down the recycled sari yarn. Use invisible thread to do this and change the stitch to a zigzag.

8. Trim round the edge (note that the piece will have shrunk slightly because of the quilting).

9. Embellish the outside of the purse with beads and sequins.

10. Place the decorated purse fabric on top of the lining fabric and pin all the way round.

11. Put your machine back to normal sewing. Attach the appliqué foot and sew all round the edge. Trim if necessary.

12. Take the fabric for the pockets and cut it into two 20.3cm (8in) squares. The remaining piece will measure 3.2 x 20.3cm (1¼ x 8in). Fold the larger pieces in half and press them. Take the thin strip, turn in 6mm (¼in) each side and press.

13. Place the zips in between the pockets, with the thin strip between the zips as shown. The zips should open from opposite ends. Pin them in place.

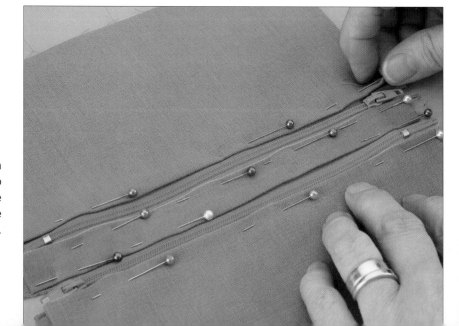

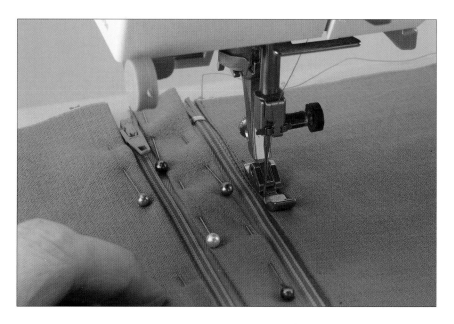

14. Change to the zipper foot and sew in the zips.

15. Place the pockets on top of the main section, wrong sides together, and pin.

16. Change back to the appliqué foot and with invisible thread top and bottom, sew all around the edge. Trim if necessary.

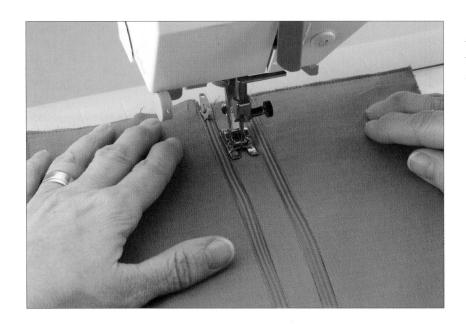

17. Still with the invisible thread top and bottom, sew down the middle of the two zips to separate the pockets.

18. To cover the raw edges, take the sari yarn and place it along the inside edge of the purse. Couch it down with invisible thread using a zigzag stitch. Repeat on the front of the purse.

19. Cover the press studs with one of the contrasting fabrics (see page 35) and attach them to the corners of the pockets.

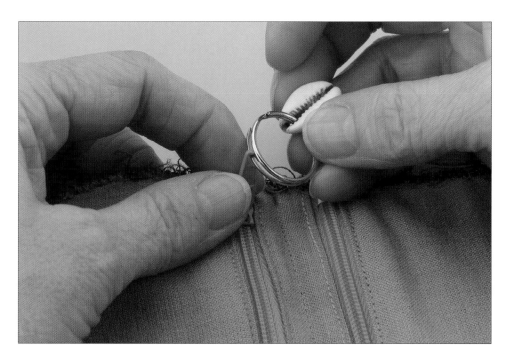

20. Attach the cowrie shells to the split rings and then to the purse zips.

The finished Indian Purse.

This alternative Indian style purse is decorated with appliqué shapes and sequins and has fabric beads in the corners.

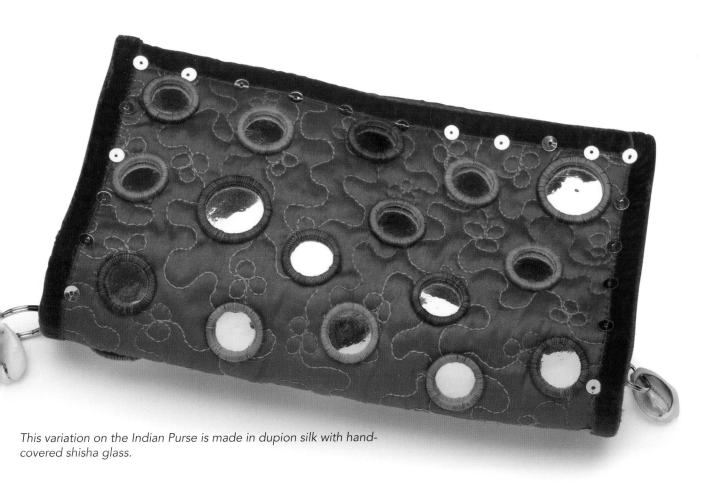

This variation on the Indian Purse is made in dupion silk with hand-covered shisha glass.

This purse was made from part of a cushion cover and has tiny bells added to the split rings.

Frilly Purse

I like to make different textures with my fabrics and lots of pleats make this purse very tactile. You do not need to measure the distance between the pleats: they will look better if they are placed randomly.

You will need

Sewing machine with walking foot, darning foot and zipper foot

Iron

Main fabric, 23 x 45.7cm (9 x 18in)

Wadding, 24 x 30.5cm (9½ x 12in)

Lining, 21.5 x 28cm (8½ x 11in)

Zip, 17.8cm (7in)

Machine thread to match top fabric, zip and lining

Fabric scissors

Pins

Large sequins

Invisible thread

Fabric adhesive spray

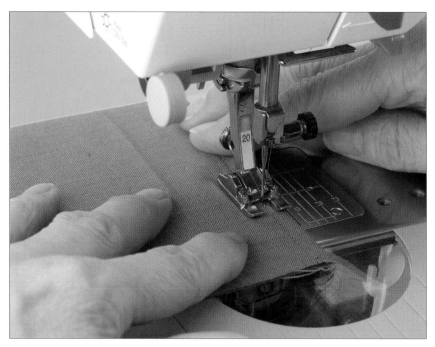

1. Take the main fabric, fold it in half and press it. Set your machine for normal sewing and sew 6mm (¼in) from the fold, using the same thread on the top and in the bobbin.

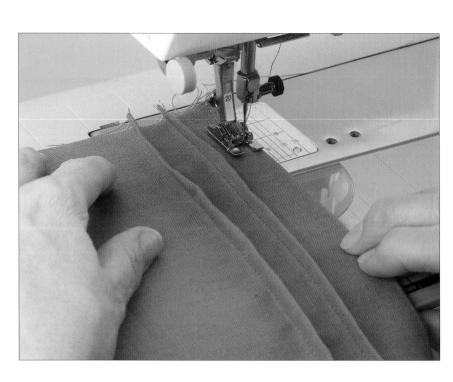

2. Make another fold beside the first one and sew as before. Continue to make a row of pleats from the centre (the first fold) to the edge.

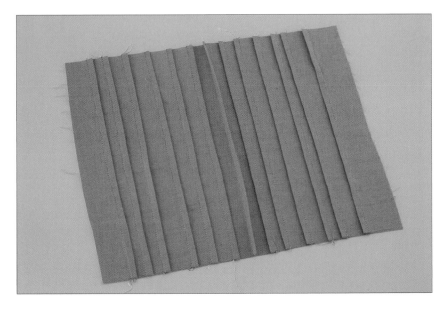

3. Now fold, press and sew pleats from the centre to the other edge. These pleats should face in the opposite direction to the first ones. Make six pleats either side of the centre fold, stopping 2.5cm (1in) from the edges. The finished piece will measure 29cm (11½in).

4. Spray the wadding with fabric adhesive and then place the outer fabric on top.

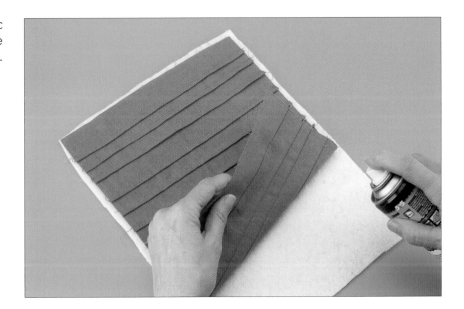

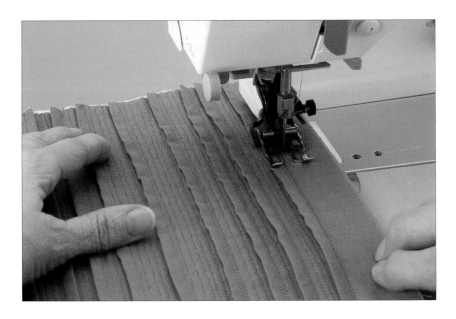

5. Attach the walking foot and using the same thread, sew rows of stitching up and down between the folds. When the sewing is complete, trim the piece down to 21.5 x 28cm (8½ x 11in).

6. Now attach the darning foot and lower the feed dogs. Put invisible thread on the top and in the bobbin. To attach the sequins, start at the edge and sew in approximately 2.5cm (1in). With the needle up, place a sequin on the fabric.

7. Hand turn the wheel so that the needle goes down in to the centre of the sequin.

8. Turn the wheel again so that the needle goes in on the far side of the sequin. Continue sewing to the next sequin position, and cover the outer fabric in this way.

Note

Do not sew sequins too close to the edges as you have to leave room for seam allowances.

9. Take the zip and place it right sides together at the top of the purse. Pin and then tack both edges of the zip.

10. Put the machine back to normal sewing and attach the zipper foot. Using thread to match the zip on the top and in the bobbin, sew down the zip. Open the zip slightly so that you will be able to turn the purse right sides out later.

11. Change back to the standard sewing foot and with thread to match the purse, sew down each side. Turn the purse right sides out.

12. Take your piece of lining and fold it in half, right sides together. Sew down each side with a 1.3cm (½in) seam allowance.

13. Turn back the top edges 1.3cm (½in) and press.

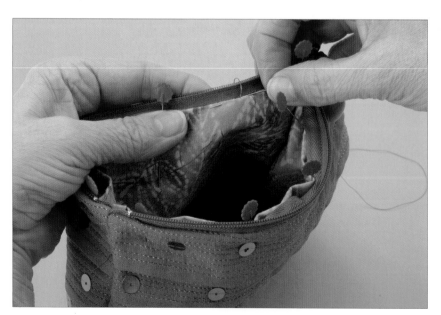

14. Pin the lining inside the purse and slip stitch it in place.

The finished Frilly Purse.

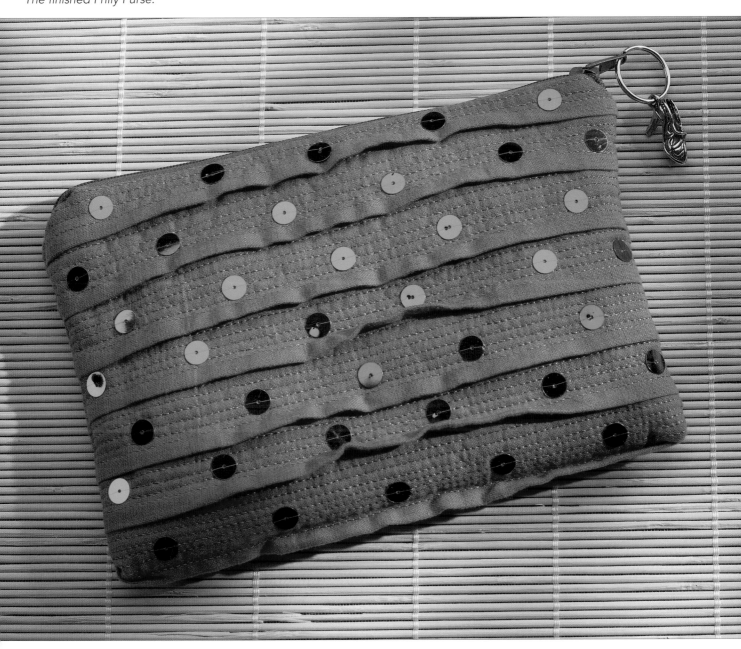

The larger, turquoise frilly purse is decorated with tiny mother-of-pearl beads and a heart charm attached to the zip. The smaller purse is made with purple dupion silk with chunky round beads added and a shoe charm on the zip.

This frilly purse in lime green is decorated with tiny turquoise beads to match the zip, and is finished with a shoe charm.

Clutch Purse

Keeping it simple is sometimes the best policy and this is a simple, classic clutch purse with free machine embroidered seed heads and beads for decoration.

You will need

Sewing machine with walking foot, darning foot and appliqué foot

Top fabric, 23 x 33cm (9 x 13in)

Wadding, 23 x 33cm (9 x 13in)

Lining, 23 x 33cm (9 x 13in)

Narrow ribbon, 99cm (39in) long, cut into three 33cm (13in) pieces

Thread to match top fabric and lining

Invisible thread

Contrasting machine quilting thread

Pins

Small beads

Set of magnetic clasps

Two pieces of heavyweight interfacing, 2.5 x 3.8cm (1 x 1½in)

Round-nosed pliers

Sharp pencil, craft knife and ruler

Fabric scissors

1. Take the top fabric and with a ruler and sharp pencil, lightly draw a line down the middle of the fabric. Draw two more lines, 6.3cm (2½in) either side of this.

2. Place the fabric on top of the wadding and position one piece of ribbon on the middle line. Pin it down.

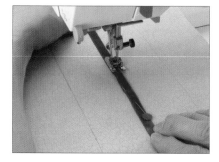

3. Attach the walking foot and with invisible thread top and bottom, sew down either side of the ribbon with a straight stitch. Repeat with the other two pieces of ribbon placed on the outer lines.

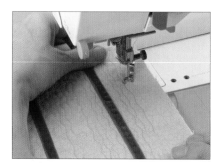

4. Change to the darning foot, lower the feed dogs and thread your machine with matching machine quilting thread. Sew up and down between the ribbons in wavy lines until the whole surface is covered.

5. Place the purse right side down and fold back 11.4cm (4½in). Pin along the fold. This will be the bottom of the purse.

Note

At this stage, measure the finished piece (it will have shrunk slightly after quilting) and if necessary cut the lining piece of fabric down to size. Put this to one side.

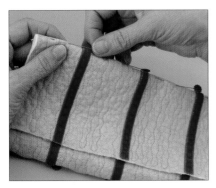

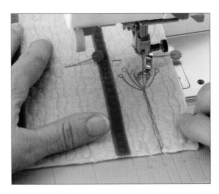

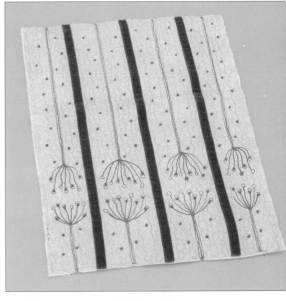

6. Fold down the flap of the purse and pin along the top fold.

7. Change to a contrasting machine quilting thread and start to free machine the seed heads. Start at the bottom of the piece, which will be the purse's flap. Take the seed heads up to the row of pins you made in step 6. This will be the top of the purse.

8. When you have finished the flap, embroider the seed heads on the rest of the purse and sew on the beads as shown.

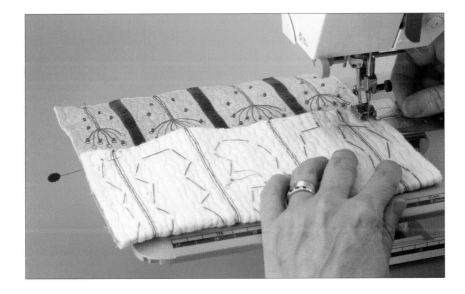

9. Change to the appliqué foot and change the thread to match the top fabric. Fold the main section of the purse, right sides together and sew the outside seams, with a 1.3cm (½in) seam allowance, leaving 1.3cm (½in) at the top for turning.

10. Change your thread to match the lining fabric and sew the outside seams of the lining in the same way, leaving 1.3cm (½in) at the top for turning.

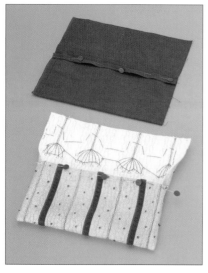

12. Place the purse with the pocket down and then place the lining, also pocket down, on top.

13. Pin then machine sew round the flap.

11. Turn the main section right sides out, but leave the lining as it is. Pin down the 1.3cm (½in) seam allowance on the main section and the lining.

14. Trim off the corners of the flap.

15. To stabilise the magnetic clasp, take one of the pieces of heavyweight interfacing and place it centrally on the top of the purse, just outside the sewn line. Machine sew it down.

Note

When choosing a lining, make sure it is not too thin, as you do not want the heavyweight interfacing to show through.

16. Turn the purse right sides out. Using a sharp craft knife, make two little cuts through both the lining and the heavyweight interfacing and insert the leg part of the magnetic clasp.

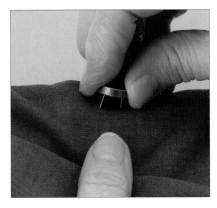

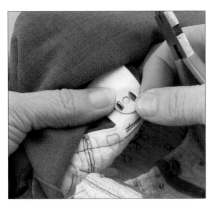

17. Fold up the flap of the purse and insert the clasp as shown.

18. Fit the back closure over the legs of the clasp.

19. Fold back the legs of the clasp to secure it, using the round-nosed pliers.

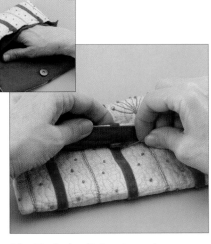

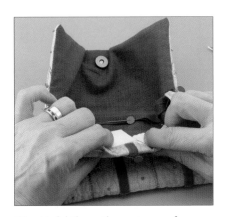

20. Tuck the lining into the purse and fold over the flap. Mark with a pin where the other part of the clasp should be.

21. Hold the other piece of heavyweight interfacing behind the place you have marked with a pin.

22. Make two little cuts through the front of the purse and the heavyweight interfacing, using the craft knife.

23. Insert the legs of the clasp through the holes as before.

24. Place the back closure over the legs of the clasp and once again turn back the legs using the round-nosed pliers.

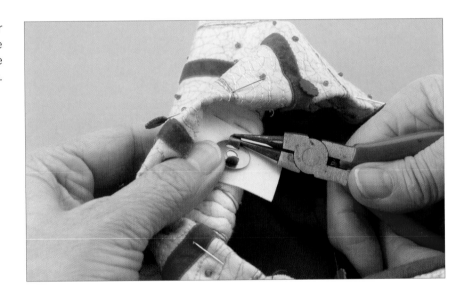

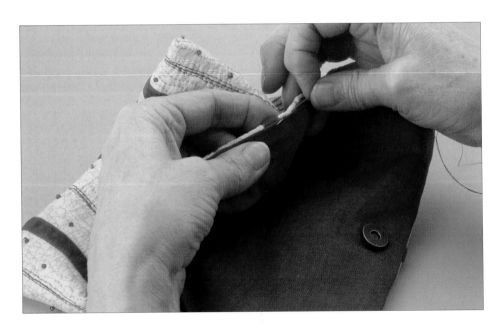

25. Finish off by pinning the lining to the front of the purse and slip stitching it in place by hand.

The finished Clutch Purse.

This clutch purse has a strap and buckle and is decorated with hand-embroidered French knots and straight stitch.

Another clutch purse, made with ribbons as shown on page 31, with a ribbon bow (see page 35).

This clutch purse has fabric ribbon couched down. The three large washers are covered with the same fabric ribbon.

Daisy Purse

One of my favourite flowers is the daisy as it cheers me up and makes me think of spring time. These little daisies are made by free machining on to heavyweight interfacing, which is an excellent way of creating your own embellishments for purses.

The template for the daisies.

The template for the purse.

You will need

Sewing machine with standard foot, darning foot and zipper foot

Top fabric, 17.8 x 40.7cm (7 x 16in)

Wadding, 17.8 x 40.7cm (7 x 16in)

Lining fabric, 17.8 x 40.7cm (7 x 16in)

20.3cm (8in) zip

Fabric adhesive spray

Freezer paper, 15.3 x 20.3cm (6 x 8in)

Iron

Fabric scissors

Needle and thread for tacking and hand sewing

Pins

Heavyweight interfacing 15.3 x 10cm (6 x 4in)

Machine quilting thread to go with top fabric, and in white and yellow

Tiny beads

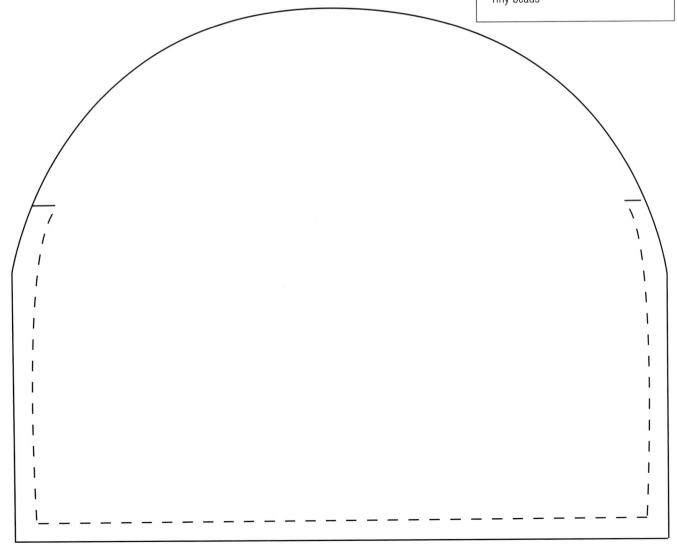

1. Cut the top fabric, wadding and lining into 17.8 x 20.3cm (7 x 8in) pieces. Put the lining pieces to one side. Take one piece of wadding and spray with the fabric adhesive spray, and place one piece of the fabric on top. Do the same with the other pieces of fabric and wadding.

2. Thread the machine with machine quilting thread, lower the feed dogs and attach the darning foot. Free machine all over both pieces of fabric and wadding with a random swirling design.

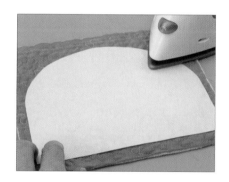

3. Put the piece of freezer paper over the template, trace it and cut it out. Place it on one of the pieces of quilted fabric, shiny side down and iron it on.

Note
You can reuse freezer paper a number of times.

4. Put the machine back to normal sewing and attach the standard foot. Sew all round the outside of the freezer paper. Repeat with the remaining piece of quilted fabric.

5. Cut out the two pieces just outside the sewn line.

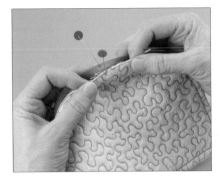

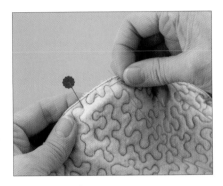

6. Place the two pieces right sides together and sew along the lines marked on the template.

7. Measure the middle of the zip and the middle of the fabric and pin them right sides together.

8. Tack in the zip.

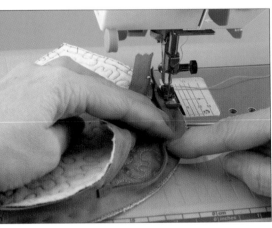

9. Change to a zipper foot and sew in the zip.

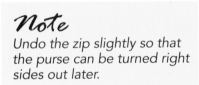

Note

Undo the zip slightly so that the purse can be turned right sides out later.

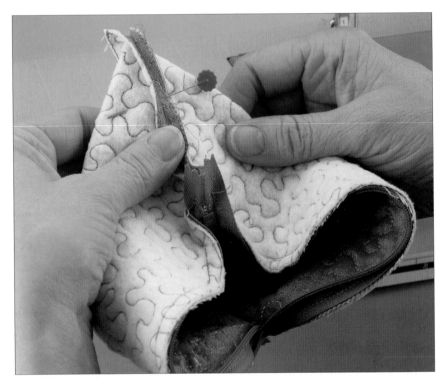

10. Fold the purse to make a triangle of one of the bottom corners as shown. Pin the purse where it measures 5cm (2in) across.

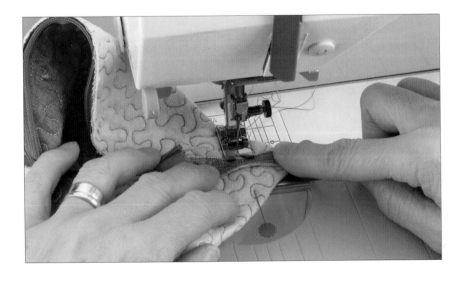

11. Change the machine back to normal sewing. Stitch across the 5cm (2in) base of the triangle. Repeat steps 10 and 11 for the other bottom corner of the purse.

12. Cut off the corner edge pieces just beyond the stitching.

13. Turn the bag right sides out.

14. Transfer the daisy template six times on to the heavyweight interfacing. Press lightly with a sharp pencil.

15. Thread the sewing machine with white thread on the top and in the bobbin. Lower the feed dogs and attach the darning foot. Start sewing the first daisy by stitching round each petal.

16. Fill in the petal with straight stitch. Repeat with all the daisies.

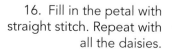

17. Change to yellow thread and fill in the middle of the daisies. Stitch round and round in circles.

18. Cut out the daisies close to the edge of the stitching. Change back to white thread and using a narrow zigzag stitch, go round all the edges of the petals to finish them off.

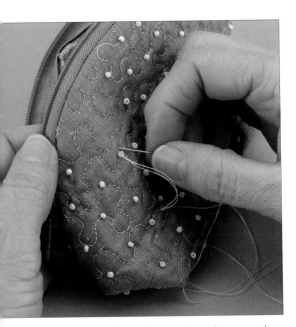

19. Sew the tiny beads on to the background on the purse.

20. Pin the daisies on to the purse and stitch them on by hand with yellow thread, leaving the petals free.

21. Take the two pieces of lining fabric and sew them together in the same way as the outside of the purse. Sew across the bottom corners and cut off the excess as for the purse.

22. Turn over the top of the lining and press it.

23. Pin the lining inside the purse and slip stitch it in place.

The finished Daisy Purse.

This version of the Daisy Purse has machine-embroidered flowers with bead centres, and is finished with a heart charm.

The purse in front has daisy-shaped buttons sewn on; the one behind has large star sequins with beads at the centres.

Box Purse

This is a very useful, chunky little purse which is covered in buttons for decoration.

You will need

Sewing machine with appliqué foot
Top fabric, 28 x 28cm
(11 x 11in)
Lining fabric, 28 x 28cm (11 x 11in)
Heavyweight interfacing, 28 x 28cm
(11 x 11in)
Fusible webbing, 28 x 28cm
(11 x 11in)
Iron
Contrasting machine thread
Needle for hand sewing
Fabric scissors
Fabric glue stick
Fifty-six buttons
Sharp pencil and ruler
Shirring elastic, 12.7cm (5in)
Small piece of sticky tape

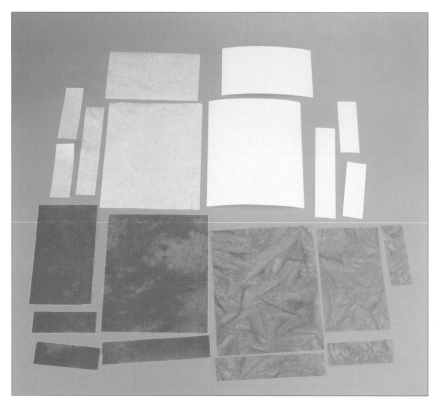

1. Take the top fabric, lining fabric, heavyweight interfacing and fusible webbing and out of each of these cut: one piece, 16 x 19cm (6¼ x 7½in); one piece, 16 x 9.5cm (6¼ x 3¾in); one piece, 16 x 3.2cm (6¼ x 1¼in); and two pieces, 9.5 x 3.2cm (3¾ x 1¼in).

2. Press the fusible webbing on to the back of the top fabric. Let it cool down and then peel off the backing.

3. Press the top fabric with the fusible webbing attached on to the heavyweight interfacing. Do this to all the pieces. Keep the lining fabric to one side for later.

4. Using a sharp pencil, draw lines 3.2cm (1¼in) apart on all the pieces, to make a grid.

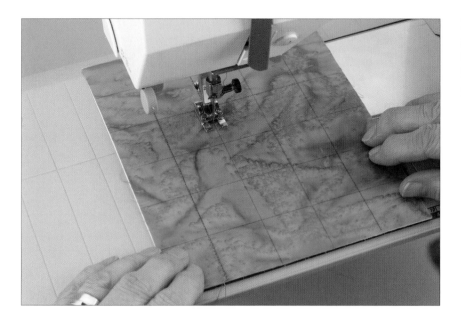

5. Set up your machine with an appliqué foot and contrasting thread. Sew along all the lines, including the edges, with a straight stitch.

6. Using doubled thread that matches the buttons, start sewing them on to the purse. On the smaller main piece, the button on the bottom middle square will be used to fasten the purse. When you sew this button on, wrap the thread round two or three times under the button so that it stands out slightly. If you do not do this, the button will be too tightly attached and the clasp might pull it off.

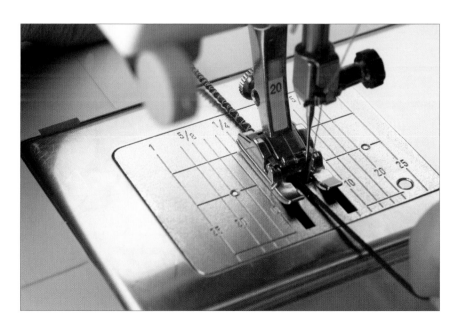

7. To cover the shirring elastic, use an appliqué foot. Set the stitch to a narrow zigzag and use a thread that matches the buttons on the top and in the bobbin. Holding the shirring elastic taut and leaving 2.5cm (1in) at either end, start to cover the elastic with the thread.

8. Sew over the shirring elastic two or three times until it is completely covered. Trim it down to 7.6cm (3in).

9. Fold the elastic into a loop and place it on the wrong side at the top of the larger main piece. Place a piece of sticky tape over it to stop it moving. With the same thread, make three or four stitches to keep the elastic in place.

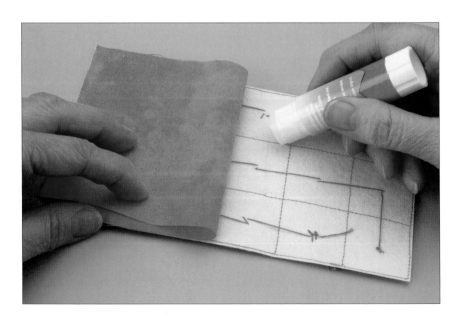

10. Take your lining pieces and the fabric glue stick and starting on the smaller main piece, rub the glue stick over the back of the interfacing and place the lining on top. Do this to all the other pieces.

11. Change the stitch to a narrow zigzag and sew all the way round all of the pieces.

12. To sew the purse together, open up the zigzag and widen the stitch. Start by sewing the base to the bottom of the larger main piece.

13. Then sew each side to the smaller main piece.

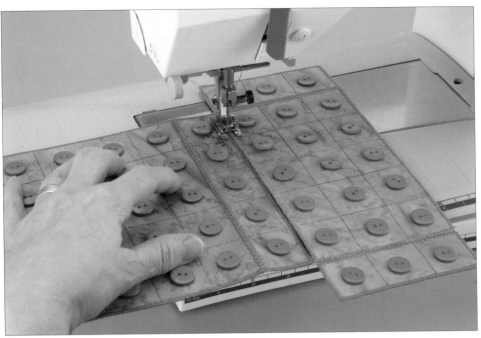

14. Then sew the smaller main piece to the base, making sure that the button used for fastening the purse is in the correct position.

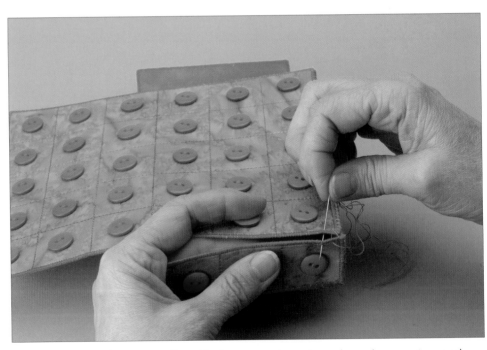

15. Lastly, thread up a needle with the same thread you have been using and sew up the remaining sides, overstitching by hand.

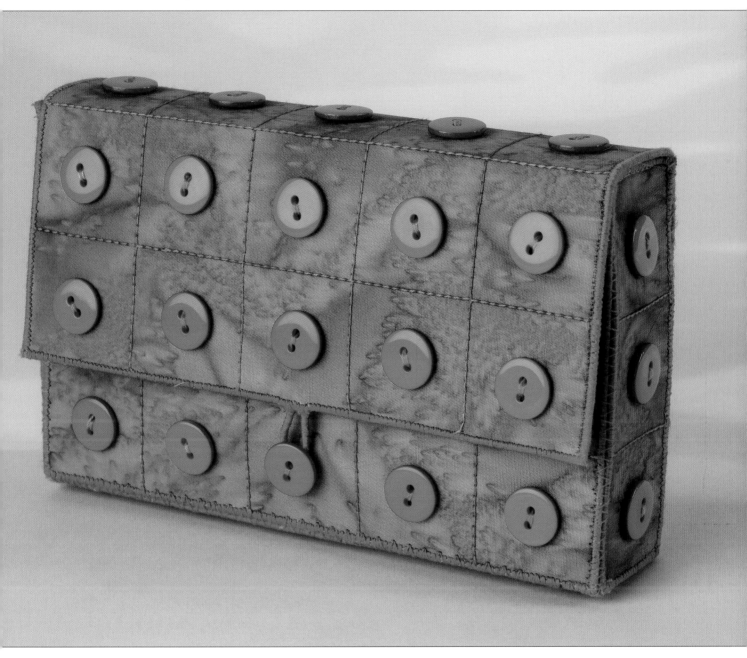

The finished Box Purse.

*The tiny box purse in front has machine-embroidered appliqué circles with buttons sewn on;
the one behind it features chunky beads sewn on by hand with embroidered straight stitches.*

This vibrant box purse is decorated by buttons in all the colours of the rainbow.

Velvet Purse

I love luxurious fabrics such as velvet and silk and wanted
to make a purse out of them that would just sit in my hand.
The magnets hidden inside the top pieces make an excellent
invisible fastening.

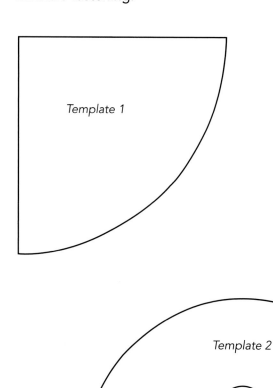

Template 1

Template 2

Template 3

You will need

Sewing machine with appliqué foot
and darning foot

For the main purse:

Two pieces of velvet, 21.6 x 15.2cm
(8½ x 6in)

Two pieces of fusible webbing,
21.6 x 15.2cm (8½ x 6in)

Two pieces of calico, 21.6 x 15.2cm
(8½ x 6in)

Two pieces of lining, 21.6 x 15.2cm
(8½ x 6in)

Variegated gimp for couching down
on the velvet

Invisible thread

Fabric scissors

Iron

Sharp pencil and ruler

Card for templates

Pins

Needle for hand sewing

For the top:

Heavyweight interfacing, 20.3 x
10cm (8 x 4in)

Fusible webbing,
20.3 x 10cm (8 x 4in)

Silk, 28 x 12.7cm (11 x 5in)

Fabric glue stick, PVA glue
and spatula

Seed beads

Two magnets

1. Starting with the main purse,
take one piece of fusible webbing
and press it on to one of the
pieces of calico.

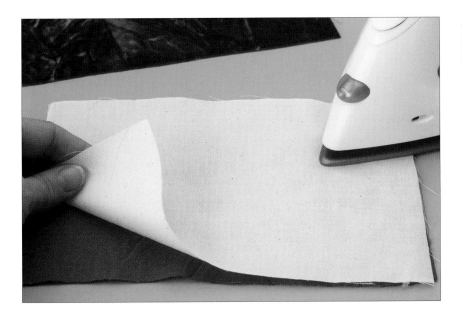

2. Peel off the paper backing and press the calico on to one of the pieces of velvet. Repeat with the remaining pieces.

3. Thread your sewing machine with invisible thread and attach a standard foot. Change the stitch to a zigzag. Starting in the middle, couch down the gimp in straight lines down the velvet. Repeat with the other piece of velvet.

4. Place both pieces right sides down, making sure that the nap is going in the same direction. Draw a pencil line down the middle. Then measure 5cm (2in) either side of the original line and draw lines on either side. Repeat for the other piece of velvet.

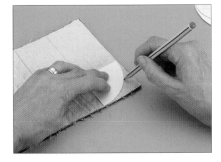

5. Put right sides together. Transfer the template 1 shape on to card. Place the template on each of the bottom corners and draw round it to make rounded corners.

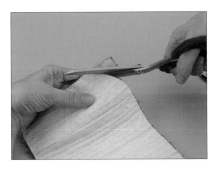

6. Cut out the rounded corners.

7. Take one of the pieces and fold it on the middle line. Place a pin 1.3cm (½in) in. Fold on the other lines and do the same. Repeat for the other piece.

8. Pin all the way round leaving 3.2cm (1¼in) free at the top either side.

9. Place the two pieces right sides together. When you have two folds facing each other, make sure you push one one way and one the other as shown.

10. Change the thread on your machine to match the velvet and sew all round the purse using a 1cm (³/₈in) seam allowance. Turn the purse right sides out.

11. Take the two pieces of lining and follow steps 4–8. Change the thread to match the lining fabric and sew all round the lining using a 1cm (³/₈in) seam allowance and leaving 3.2cm (1¼in) free at the top either side.

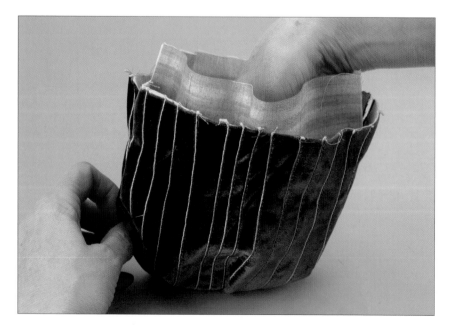

12. Place the lining in the purse.

13. Pin all round the top.

14. Turn in the side seams and slip stitch them down.

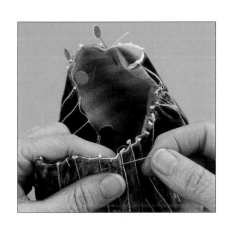

15. Thread a needle with the thread that matches the velvet and using it double, running stitch across the top of each side of the purse.

16. Gather each side of the purse until it measures 7.6cm (3in) across.

17. Transfer template 2 on to card, place it on top of the heavyweight interfacing and draw round it four times. Cut the shapes out. Do the same on the fusible webbing.

18. Transfer template 3 on to card, place it on the silk and draw round it four times with a dark pencil on light fabric or a light pencil on dark fabric. Cut out the silk shapes.

19. Place one piece of fusible webbing on to a piece of the silk and press it with an iron.

20. Peel off the backing and place the silk on top of a piece of the heavyweight interfacing. Press with the silk uppermost, since the heat of the iron cannot penetrate through the heavyweight interfacing.

21. Thread a needle with thread that matches the silk and then gather round the edge and pull the thread tight. Sew two or three little stitches to finish off.

22. Use a fabric glue stick along the base of the semicircle of heavyweight interfacing.

23. Fold over the silk edge and stick it down. Repeat steps 19–23 to make four semicircular pieces.

24. Lower the feed dogs and attach a darning foot. Using your chosen thread, free machine all over two of the pieces in a swirling pattern.

25. Sew beads on to each of these free machined pieces with matching thread, being careful not to go too close to the edge.

26. Take the two remaining pieces. Put a small amount of PVA glue on the back of each magnet and place one on the back of each piece, referring to template 2. Leave until dry.

27. Change your machine back to normal sewing with an appliqué foot and place invisible thread on the top and in the bobbin. Take one of each of the top pieces. Place wrong sides together and sew all round the semicircle, really close to the edge. Do the same with the other two pieces.

28. Place one of the tops over one side of the gathered main purse, pin it in place and sew along the edge. Do the same to the other side.

The finished Velvet Purse.

This sumptuous velvet purse has tiny buttons sewn on and is finished with a handmade brooch (see page 34).

This purse was made with hand-dyed velvet. The pattern on the top was machine embroidered.

The threads couched down on this velvet purse were hand-dyed. The top is made from dupion silk.

Index